ROAD SIGNS to FREEDOM

Fixing Your Eyes on Jesus

Jonathan Hogan

Road Signs to Freedom

Jonathan Hogan Ministries, 2015
www.JonathanHogan.org

Front Cover image: © www.123rf.com/nexusplexus
Cover Design: Elizabeth Little, Hyliaan Graphic Design
Interior: The Author's Mentor, www.littleronipublishers.com

ISBN-13: 978-1517791704
ISBN-10: 1517791707
Also available in eBook

PUBLISHED IN THE UNITED STATES OF AMERICA

Acknowledgments

I would like to acknowledge my wife Melody for allowing me the time to work on this book. Your counsel and encouragement have been invaluable during its creation. I love you! I would also like to thank my children Josiah and Judah. You are both so young and yet you are an inspiration for me to keep moving toward God. Thank you to all the members of my family for the many years of support you have given me. I want to thank my mother for helping with the grammar issues in this document. I would like to thank Ellen Sallas for editing and putting the book together. Thank you to all my friends who have encouraged my ministry. I also want to thank all the ministers and teachers who have taught me the word of God. Even if we disagreed, your teaching encouraged me to go deeper with Jesus. Lastly, I want to thank you the reader for getting this book, I pray that your relationship with God grows deeper over this next season of your life.

Dedication

This book is dedicated to the Lord Jesus Christ. I have tried to point towards you in every chapter of it. I pray that you will use it for your kingdom.

I also wish to dedicate this book to the weary. You have stood on the front lines for so many years. My prayer is that this book will bring resurrection life to you again.

Contents

ROAD SIGNS TO FREEDOM

Fixing Your Eyes on Jesus

Introduction

Road Signs to Freedom is a collection of teachings designed to point to Jesus while revealing spiritual hindrances. Each chapter centers on a specific theme or teaching of Christ designed to remove false mindsets and lay proper foundations. As our minds are renewed by the spirit of Christ, we are transformed and freed from the yokes of slavery. As we are freed from slavery, our spirits can take flight into the heights of God's love and freedom.

So many people, clergy and laity, have shared with me that they feel they are floundering in their spiritual life. Many of them desire to be a blessing to others and grow closer to the Lord. But it seems like their desires are frustrated and their dreams couldn't seem further away. On the outside they appear to have it all together, but on the inside they feel like Bilbo Baggins, "Like butter scraped over too much bread." This path of searching and frustration is starting to seem all too familiar. Much of what I am sharing will benefit the weary.

The truths addressed in this book are like road signs that ministers and lay people will need. Each road sign points to the source of our freedom, Jesus. This book is not intended to be an end-all compilation of every single road sign one can come across. Rather, it is a collection of examples and teachings from the life and ministry of Jesus that have helped me in my own journey. Each chapter is its own standalone teaching, however many of the teachings do build on each other. Each teaching is not meant to represent the fullness of all there is to say on a particular subject. They are meant to briefly point out areas where our focus tends to waiver.

The point of our lives is relationship with Jesus. He is our peace, our love, our rest and our goodness, etc. He is the one that we must look to. If our focus waivers from the Lord Jesus we can find ourselves going off course in a dramatic way. Having our heart permanently focused on the Lord is one way that we can stay on the right path without being diverted down lesser roads that aren't the road the Lord has for us. The ultimate road sign to freedom is the Lord Jesus Christ. As we keep our focus on him our course will remain steady.

The point of our lives is relationship with Jesus.

The content in these chapters is somewhat diverse. Some of the material may seem overly simplified, while other portions may be thoroughly challenging. I recommend that you read the book through one time and then go back and ask the Lord to give you his thoughts concerning the parts that are challenging. This book will be good to have on hand as a resource for quick review.

I hope that you will enjoy *Road Signs to Freedom.* Many of the lessons I've learned are in its pages and I hope they will bless you on your journey. Even if you ultimately disagree with me on an interpretation, it should provide an opportunity for you to begin reconciling certain issues in your life.

My writing style is somewhat blunt and that is because I feel like I can't afford to waste this opportunity. If you read anything that you find offensive, please note that it was not my goal to try to be offensive but rather to clearly state what I believe to be true. After all, it is the truth that sets us free.

~Jonathan Hogan

Chapter 1
Jesus

...and thou shalt call his name JESUS
Matthew 1:21

The highest life we can live is experienced in a deep abiding relationship with the Lord Jesus Christ. Jesus is our all-in-all, in all of our being. He is a son, a friend, a lover and a savior. Jesus is our reward, our joy, our peace, our shield and our life.

Jesus doesn't just show the way, he *is* the way. He shows the way, leads the way and when we reach the end we find Him there, too. The way is not a thing you do or something you build; it is a person who is built inside of you.

Jesus is our peace; he is our rest, our stillness and ever increasing bliss. There is no greater peace than to rest in the presence of the one who *is* peace. A million angry people cannot undo one drop of his peace. His peace calms our storms first and then reaches beyond the confines of us and calms the storms around us. After all, he is the King who walked on the stormy Sea of Galilee. The bliss of abiding in him undoes all of our cares and anxieties.

He is small enough for a child and yet large enough for all creation. He walks amongst the rich and dances with the poor. He sings among the saints and lifts the head of sinners. He is the humblest of kings.

He heals the sick, raises the dead and lifts us up to sit with him. Sickness cannot last in his presence and he is so full of life that all our emotional and physical deaths revert back to life in his presence. For He only knows how to conduct resurrections.

In Jesus we live, move and have our being. The life we live is Jesus, the movements we make are Jesus, and our being itself is Jesus.

He is the healing and health we seek. He is the joy we desire. Nothing exists outside of Him, and nothing would ever want to if the result of doing so could be known.

He is the way to Heaven and He is heaven itself. All of our self-made hells are turned into heaven when placed in his hands.[1] Every move he makes, song he sings, teaching he gives or life he changes reveals more of heaven. Heaven comes to earth through Jesus. As he lives in us, heaven comes to earth through us.

Learning to live in Jesus is our ultimate quest. He doesn't operate like the world operates, so it's a different kind of life. We can gain everything and yet without him, find that we have lost everything. We can also lose everything *for him* and realize we have gained everything. Gaining the Lord is everything. **He is our everything.** He is worth paying any price. For he is the pearl of great price hidden in the field and it's worth it to give up everything in order to have it.

---

[1] Moseley, J. Rufus. Perfect Everything. Saint Paul : Macalester Park Publishing Company, 1949. p. 20.

He isn't distant; he is closer than the air we breathe. We can rest at his feet and we can sit at his table. For all provision and nourishment comes from him. All light comes from him. Darkness has nothing to do with him because there is nothing of darkness within him to claim. There is no shadow of turning within him.

Jesus is our brother and in him we are sons of God. We are co-heirs with the one who is heir to everything. There is nothing Jesus is to receive from his father that we can't also enjoy with him. He goes before us and gains everything and then turns around and gives everything to us. Those who do the same find themselves acting like him.

> *Jesus doesn't just show the way, he is the way.*

In him, we find ourselves washing feet, holding back the tears of the backslidden, and annoying the self-righteous. The only way we can do all of these things is to look to him and abide in him. As we look to him, our nature is changed and we take on his light and lose all our darkness. There must be nothing in us that would want to show ourselves superior to the one we are with. We must lose sarcasm, self-righteousness, cynicism, and pride. With them we may be able to sound smart but in his economy, the superior loses.

He rejoices when we humble ourselves before him. He shouts when we turn to him. Even if we have just torn down the stars out of spite, when we turn back to him heaven acts as if we've just hung the moon.

The life we live in Jesus is the highest life we can live but grows by first surrendering to Him. The place of surrender is the humblest and lowest of places. Meeting him right where we are, in the reality of all we are going through. Right where you are this moment, go there and you'll find he is there waiting for you.

Chapter 2
The Beam in Your Own Eye

And why beholdest thou the mote that is in thy brother's eye, but considerest not the beam that is in thine own eye?

Or how wilt thou say to thy brother, Let me pull out the mote out of thine eye; and, behold, a beam is in thine own eye?

Thou hypocrite, first cast out the beam out of thine own eye; and then shalt thou see clearly to cast out the mote out of thy brother's eye.
Matthew 7:3-5

There were two trees in the Garden of Eden that we all must come to terms with. The first tree was called the tree of life and was the tree God invited man to eat of. This tree represented relationship with God where we look to him as our sufficiency. The second tree was the tree of the knowledge of good and evil. This tree represented humanism, or man looking to himself, his own ability and his own definition of right and wrong.

When Adam and Eve ate the fruit of the tree of knowledge, they were forced to start measuring the good against the evil within themselves. Before they had eaten of the tree of knowledge, they were secured by their relationship with God. By eating of the tree of knowledge, they were effectively saying that they wanted to secure their own standing before God by understanding and performing good and evil (right and wrong).

The results of eating the tree of knowledge are two things that have plagued humanity ever since: shame and self-righteousness. When you are forced to weigh the good and the evil within yourself, if the good is presently outweighing the evil then you are righteous according to your own definition. This is called self-righteousness. If the evil is presently outweighing the good this results in shame, or what Adam and Eve were feeling when they hid.[2]

In order to get man back into paradise after the fall, God needed to help him get routed back to the tree of life. When the time came for Jesus to walk the earth, one of the ways he referred to himself was "***life***."

> **Jesus saith unto him, I am the way, the truth, and the life: no man cometh unto the Father, but by me.**
>
> John 14:6

By referring to himself as "the life" Jesus was saying I am the tree of life. In fact, Galatians 3:13 refers to the cross as a tree:

> **Christ hath redeemed us from the curse of the law, being made a curse for us: for it is written, Cursed *is* every one that hangeth on a tree.**

---

[2] Joyner, Rick. There Were Two Trees in the Garden. Fort Mills : Morning Star Publications, 1985. pp. 7-15. ISBN 978-1-929371-55-6; 1-929371-55-1.

Through this we can see that Jesus took the effects of the tree of knowledge on himself and then went to the cross (the tree). Because of Christ's finished work, at the cross, we are now free to receive the Lord Jesus Christ, the tree of life.

The fruit of the tree of life can be seen when we choose to turn to the cross of Jesus.

Though we are free to eat of the tree of life, humanity still struggles to tell the difference between these two trees. One of the primary areas that humanity still struggles with these two trees is in the area of **bitterness**.

When an individual is wronged, one of the sure signs that they are eating from the wrong tree is the presence of bitterness over the event. When someone does something hurtful to us, there are only two places that we can turn. We can turn to the Lord Jesus, the tree of life, or we can turn to the tree of the knowledge of good and evil. Whichever tree we turn to will determine the results. A tree only brings forth fruit after its kind.

> **And God said, Let the earth bring forth grass, the herb yielding seed, *and* the fruit (tree) yielding fruit *after his kind*, whose seed *is* in itself, upon the earth: and it was so.**
>
> Genesis 1:11

The fruit of the tree of life can be seen when we choose to turn to the cross of Jesus. When we turn to the cross of Jesus, the result is we lay down our own righteousness for the Lord's righteousness. We lay down our own life for the Lord. If the result of turning to the tree of knowledge is shame and self-righteousness, the result of turning to the tree of life is grace and the righteousness of God in Christ Jesus.

The reality is that bitterness can only live in the potting soil of self-righteousness. If I am holding on to bitterness, what I am really holding onto is my concept of what is right and wrong, i.e. the tree of knowledge. By holding onto that concept, I'm holding on to the idea that I am owed something. I'm holding on to the idea that I am somehow above you, while you are beneath me. This is nothing more, nothing less, then self-righteousness. The truth of our righteousness can be seen in Isaiah 64:6

> **...and all our righteousnesses *are* as filthy rags.**

Of course all our righteousness is filthy, look at the results of it. The result of our own righteousness is a bitterness that poisons our own soul.

The only antidote to self-righteousness is to turn to the cross of Jesus. By turning to the cross of Christ, we can receive a righteousness that is a free gift.

> **For he hath made him *to be* sin for us, who knew no sin; that we might be made the righteousness of God in him.**
>
> 2 Corinthians 5:21

The truth is that all true righteousness is a free gift of God. When we truly see this about God's righteousness, when we truly turn to the cross of Christ, we see that we are no greater and no lesser than our brother who has wronged us.

To be free from the poison of bitterness, we must turn to the cross. It's at the cross that we can finally let go of that which we believe we are owed. It's at the cross that we receive forgiveness from God; that is the same forgiveness God gives everyone else. Since I am no greater and no lesser than my brother or sister who has wronged me, I realize that I and my brother are the same before God. My brother and I both need God's forgiveness. My brother and I both need God's grace. My brother and I both need God's salvation. At the cross of Christ Jesus, bitterness cannot stay.

Here is a parable for you to consider. Bitterness is like a man who volunteers to be a prisoner. While he is in his jail, a man comes with a key and says, "I have the key to your freedom and I will give it to you." The man in prison replies, "No thank you, sir. You see, it is you that are in prison, not me."

Chapter 3
A Long Way Off

I will arise and go to my father, and will say unto him,
Father, I have sinned against heaven, and before thee,
And am no more worthy to be called thy son: make me as
one of thy hired servants.
Luke 15:18-19

One of the most stirring passages in the Gospels is a parable of Jesus known as the parable of the prodigal son. This parable has been used in sermon illustrations, books, and retreats for as long as I can remember. I confess that this parable has captivated me for many years, and has come to have a personal importance in my life.

The ancient story I'm speaking of goes like this:

> **And the younger of them said to *his* father, Father, give me the portion of goods that falleth *to me.* And he divided unto them *his* living.**
>
> **And not many days after the younger son gathered all together, and took his journey into a far country, and there wasted his substance with riotous living.**

And when he had spent all, there arose a mighty famine in that land; and he began to be in want.

And he went and joined himself to a citizen of that country; and he sent him into his fields to feed swine.

And he would fain have filled his belly with the husks that the swine did eat: and no man gave unto him.

And when he came to himself, he said, How many hired servants of my father's have bread enough and to spare, and I perish with hunger!

I will arise and go to my father, and will say unto him, Father, I have sinned against heaven, and before thee,

And am no more worthy to be called thy son: make me as one of thy hired servants.

And he arose, and came to his father. But when he was yet a great way off, his father saw him, and had compassion, and ran, and fell on his neck, and kissed him.

And the son said unto him, Father, I have sinned against heaven, and in thy sight, and am no more worthy to be called thy son.

But the father said to his servants, Bring forth the best robe, and put *it* on him; and put a ring on his hand, and shoes on *his* feet:

And bring hither the fatted calf, and kill *it;* and let us eat, and be merry:

For this my son was dead, and is alive again; he was lost, and is found.

Luke 15:12-24

Most of the teaching that I've heard on this parable seems to focus on the love the father had for the son.

This is good since I believe the purpose of the passage is to focus on the love our heavenly father has for all of us as his children. However, I did not fully understand the height of the father's love for his son until I saw the depth of the son's sin.

The first step the son took towards the depth of sin was having no love for his father. The story begins with the son asking for his inheritance. This is a major slap in the face to the child's father. The child is effectively saying it would be better if you were dead so that I can have my inheritance. To our utter dismay, the father grants his request and gives him his inheritance. It would seem that, like the death the Lord Jesus had to suffer, the father was willing to endure being dead to the son in order to do a work of love in his child.

Whenever we choose a life of sin we are actually choosing to distance ourselves from the love of God.

A symptom that the son was stepping into the depths of sin is seen in his traveling to a "far off land." It seems that the Lord Jesus is likening a life of sin unto a distance that we create between us and God. Whenever we choose a life of sin we are actually choosing to distance ourselves from the love of God. Some people believe that because they sin or make some mistake that it is God who is distancing himself from them. The result of believing this lie is a general feeling of unworthiness. The truth is, like the prodigal son, we tend to travel to a "far off land" only when we doubt the love of our Father. The Father never leaves us; we leave him.

After the son fell even further, by using everything the father had given him for selfish purposes, he ends up where all distance from God leads us, the pigpen.

Whenever we doubt the Father's love, the only place it can truly lead us is the pigpen. The pigpen is where we fully encounter what distance from God has created in our lives. It's in the pigpen that we are hungry, tired and weighed down. It is in the pigpen, where we fully reap the fruit of our decision to doubt God's love. The fruit of this decision is a slave mentality.

We see the slave mentality, when the prodigal son says:

> **How many hired servants of my father's have bread enough and to spare.**

The son is thinking if I could just be a slave in my father's house, I could have food. We see that the end result of life in the pigpen is the mindset of slavery. The Scriptures talk about this mindset of slavery in Romans 8:15 (italics mine).

> **For ye have not received the spirit of bondage (slavery) again to fear; but ye have received the Spirit of adoption, whereby we cry, Abba, Father.**

The Scripture says that we have not received the Spirit of slavery because God has not given us that spirit. It is we who embrace that spirit when we move away from God.

It is here, when the son reaches rock bottom that he "comes to his senses." This is the point where my teaching on the prodigal son is a little bit different than what most people teach. Most people teach that it was here the son realized his error and his need to repent. However, I do not believe that the son was truly repentant at this point. If he was, the story would depict our repentance as having nothing to do with the father. I believe that the son, "coming to his senses," is an even further example of his doubting his father's love.

When the son has his moment of realization, he says to himself:

> **I will arise and go to my father, and will say unto him, Father, I have sinned against heaven, and before thee, and am no more worthy to be called thy son: make me as one of thy hired servants.**

At this point, I don't believe the son was truly ready to be reconciled to the father's love. If he were ready to be reconciled to his father's love, he would not have referred to himself as a "servant." Since he is operating in a slave mentality, I believe that it is his motivation to attempt to manipulate his father's affection in order to be made a slave. It seems more likely that the son's motivation was more or less just to keep from going hungry. This depicts the selfish actions of a spiritual slave.

It is here that we reach the end of the story. The son sets course for home. And the story tells us that, "while he was still a long ways off," the father took off running towards the son in order to greet him. The truth is we cannot repent until the Father meets us in the midst of our sin. For this, he meets us while we are still a long ways off. The son launches into his manipulative pre-recorded speech and it is here that I believe the son realizes the love of his father for the first time. It is here the father says:

> **But the father said to his servants, Bring forth the best robe, and put *it* on him; and put a ring on his hand, and shoes on *his* feet:**

> **and bring hither the fatted calf, and kill *it;* and let us eat, and be merry: For this my son was dead, and is alive again; he was lost, and is found**

The scandalous love of the father does something that our religious minds have such trouble understanding. The father runs out to meet the son, whose motive for repenting isn't even pure, and he lavishes his son with his love. The father hears his son launch into the speech that he's cooked up and he chooses to ignore it and lavish his love on his son. He knows that unless the son has a revelation of his love the son can never truly repent. For that, the father had to forgive him even when his motivation for forgiveness was selfish. It was at this point the son was truly able to repent. It was at this point the father broke the power of his son's slavery mindset. The height of God's love, or any person's love, is always seen in the depth of what they will forgive. Repentance is accomplished when the revelation of God's love has replaced the issue of sin in our life. Without God, we can't even repent correctly. The Scriptures teach

> **Or despisest thou the riches of his goodness and forbearance and longsuffering; not knowing that the goodness of God leadeth thee to repentance?**
>
> Romans 2:4

If you are struggling with areas of sin and shame that seem to resurface again and again, know that when you turn to the Lord, even if you're ashamed to have to turn to the Lord over the same issue, it is at this point Father sees you though you are a long ways off. It is at this point the Father starts running. When you're crippled by fear and being destroyed by shame, know that the father is running towards you. When you are afraid of what God would say to you and you want to launch into a speech meant to earn you some measure of grace, lay it down and let the love of God embrace you and remove all the pain away. The love of God is free and the grace of God is free. It is only by accepting what is free that we can repent from the heart and not from a desire to manipulate God. Repentance is complete when the love of God has replaced the shame of sin. And the love of God is so great that repentance starts with him.

Chapter 4
Repent for the Kingdom of Heaven is at Hand

From that time Jesus began to preach, and to say, Repent: for the kingdom of heaven is at hand.
Matthew 4:17

Do you remember what it was like as a child when your parents went out to dinner without you? Maybe you were excited at first to have that feeling of freedom. Like the movie *Home Alone*, maybe you were ready to party hard leaving mass destruction in the house. Most children, excited or not, eventually end up getting a little upset when their parents leave for a while. Maybe you did when you were little and a baby sitter had to tell you "everything is going to be ok, they'll be home soon." This is the type of mindset the people had when Jesus first began his public ministry.

When Jesus began his public ministry, the scriptures say he went around teaching, "repent for the kingdom of heaven is at hand." The Scriptures imply that he went around and taught this regularly.

> ***From that time Jesus began to preach*, and to say, Repent: for the kingdom of heaven is at hand.**
>
> Matthew 4:17

Notice how Matthew writes, "From that time on." The implication is that this message of Jesus was a foundational message that he took with him to many different places he ministered.

The Scriptures tell us that Jesus is our foundation and that no other foundation can be laid except that foundation which has already been laid.

> **For other foundation can no man lay than that is laid, which is Jesus Christ.**
>
> 1 Corinthians 3:11

If Jesus' first message to the people was "repent for the kingdom of heaven is at hand," then we need to make certain that we understand what Jesus was referring to when he said it. Since Jesus himself was the foundation, we can assume that this foundational teaching of Christ Jesus is foundational for all of us.

Perhaps the most common interpretation of this Scripture is the one that focuses on the issue of sin. Christians in western culture have been taught to polarize to the issue of sin and guilt. Most Christians have been taught that they need to repent until they can't think of anything left to repent of. People are taught that their guilt separates them from God and in order to be close to God again they need to repent to remove the distance. Certainly, the Scriptures do teach the repentance of sin, that fact is not in dispute. The question is whether this interpretation is the most accurate understanding of what Jesus was trying to communicate here.

The inauguration of Jesus' ministry came at an odd time in biblical history. Between the Book of Malachi, the last book in the Old Testament, and Matthew 1:1, there was a period of time I am calling the 400 silent years. During this period, there was not much communication from God to man. For a long time, God had been speaking to humanity through the prophets and yet during this time it seemed as though there were no prophets to speak for God. Think about what that must have felt like. God had been moving for centuries, doing things like parting seas and turning rivers to blood. And then, God was silent. How would you feel? Maybe like a child whose parent has gone away for a while.

> No matter what you may feel at any time, God is not far away.

The most common reaction that people have whenever it seems like God isn't coming through for them is the belief that God is distant. I've lost track of how many people I've counseled who come to me with the belief that God has "abandoned them." I've talked with people who have been hit in their finances, hit in their family relationships, and hit in their business with all sorts of problems. And the most common element between them is this idea "why does it seem like God is so distant." This type of belief system is likely what the people had felt around the inauguration of Jesus' ministry.

Keeping all of this in mind, let's take a closer look at what Jesus actually said. The first thing Jesus said was to "repent." As I've already mentioned, most people think of the word repent and they automatically think about some active sin they need to ask Jesus to forgive them for. There is nothing wrong with repenting for active sin. However, the meaning of the word repent goes much deeper than this. The implication of the word repent is to do a 180° turn. You were going one direction, now it's time to go a different direction; this change is called repentance. The act of repentance begins in the heart and mind where you get to make a decision to want to go with God. Another way of putting it is to say that repentance means, "think differently." Repent doesn't just mean to go through some verbal recitation to God with the fact that you're sorry, it means to change your thinking.

The next part of the phrase is, "for the kingdom of heaven is at hand." In order to understand this part we need to know what the kingdom of heaven is. To put it simply, the kingdom of heaven is the domain that God resides over. The kingdom of heaven is where God is present. A few aspects of the kingdom of heaven are:

> **For the kingdom of God is not meat and drink; but righteousness, and peace, and joy in the Holy Ghost.**
>
> Romans 14:7

The last part of the Scripture says that the kingdom of God is, "in the Holy Ghost." The Holy Spirit is the person of the Godhead that Jesus sent to us. Concerning the Holy Spirit, Jesus said I will send you "another comforter." The Holy Spirit is what we often refer to when we talk about the presence of God.

To start pulling together what we've been discussing, we need to take these two ideas and put them together. What was Jesus saying? Jesus was effectively saying, **change the way you think, God is very close**. Why did Jesus give this teaching? It's simple, people have the tendency to think of God as being far away. The implication of this teaching does not seem to be that everybody he was talking to had to get right with God or God was going to burn them alive. The implication is that God is close to them. Jesus went around teaching, "repent for the kingdom of heaven is at hand." In most places Jesus went, he would teach and he would also perform all kinds of miracles.

So, he would teach this and then start healing the sick, raising the dead, cleansing the lepers and casting out demons. It would seem that the revelation that God is close rather than far away, was all that Jesus wanted to give to start his miraculous public ministry. So, one of the keys to a miraculous encounter based relationship with Jesus, is the belief that God is close to you.

Take a few minutes and think about where in your relationship with God you have felt distant. Is it because of a mistake that you made? If so, I would tell you that it was Adam and Eve who went and hid. It wasn't God who ran away and said I can't have anything to do with you. Is it because things don't seem to be working out quite like you plan? If so, realize that just before Jesus came on the scene things were not looking like everybody had planned. However, regardless of the circumstance, God the father, the Lord Jesus and the Holy Spirit are all very close to you. When you slip or life seems to fall in a hole, ask God to help you avoid the temptation that Adam and Eve yielded to; the temptation to run and hide. The truth is, it is *we* that try to build distance with God. It is the lie of the enemy that we believe that makes us feel unworthy to come before God just as we are. Jesus never rebuked anyone who came in the honesty and openness of who they really were. That's because Jesus didn't come to condemn the world but to save the world.

If you feel distant from God, take a few minutes and ask the Father to come in and began removing that distance. Ask him to come in and remove the lies of the enemy and replace those lies with the truth of who he wants to be for you: a loving God who is very near. If you feel distance from God, "repent for the kingdom of heaven is at hand. Child, change the way you think, I am very close to you."

Chapter 5
Listen to Him

While he yet spake, behold, a bright cloud overshadowed them: and behold a voice out of the cloud, which said, This is my beloved Son, in whom I am well pleased; hear ye him.
Matthew 17:5

The desire to build has been placed in all of humanity. This desire originates in the Lord's command to, "**fill the earth and subdue it**" (Genesis 1:28). With the instruction to subdue, there is a tendency in humanity to want to build empires. In other words, post the Fall of Humanity in Genesis chapter 3, there is the tendency to build that which God is not building. We need to note that, "**except the LORD build the house, they labour in vain that build it**," (Psalms 127:1). It would seem that humanity, without God, still attempts to "subdue," even if it is attempting to subdue that which belongs to God. Attempting to subdue God's kingdom or God's people is not the instruction; the instruction was to subdue the earth. This root issue is how many of God's people fall from a presence of God (relational) focus to a functional or task-oriented approach to their spirituality.

The latter may allow us to build successful Christian ministries, but it is ultimately a distraction from the Lord.

The task-oriented approach to Christianity focuses on what we can do for God. This is how much of Christianity thinks concerning ministry. People often focus their attention on the development of committees, boards and sub ministries in order to attempt to build their empire higher. In these models people are burdened with tasks and functions that they are supposed to perform "for God" and man.

The presence or relational approach to Christianity focuses on what God does for us. This more accurately reflects the nature of the Gospel. Jesus was the one who went to the cross and he is the one we listen to for direction. When we learn to listen to God and move by the leading of the Holy Spirit, there is an ease about our ministry because it is the Lord that is moving through us rather than we who are trying to do something for him. In this, we see the Lord carrying the burden for us, while we focus on loving and leaning into him.

The best illustration I know of relational Christianity (presence-oriented) over task-oriented is the Mountain of Transfiguration experience (Matthew 17). In this account, Jesus goes on top of a mountain with Peter, James and John. While there, Jesus is transfigured, meaning he began to glow with radiant light all about him. Additionally, a cloud of glory surrounded Jesus and the three disciples. Finally, Jesus ends up speaking with the deceased prophets Elijah and Moses.

Everything in this experience suggests a relational focus. He picks several disciples, with whom he was closest, to go on top of the mountain with him. Once he arrived, he began to have a powerful intimacy encounter with the presence of the Most High God.

Additionally he was allowed what Scriptures call, the communion of the saints, with Elijah and Moses. And Peter James and John got to see the Lord transfigured.

I believe the reason Peter, James and John could come up on the mountain with Jesus was so that they would see him as he truly was. The more intimate we are with the Lord, the more revelation of him we carry. In a since, we all get to be transfigured, however the true Transfiguration is us being allowed to see the Lord Jesus as he is. For example, the Scriptures say:

> **But we all, with open face beholding as in a glass the glory of the Lord, are changed into the same image from glory to glory, *even* as by the Spirit of the Lord.**
>
> 2 Corinthians 3:18

It is by seeing the Christ that we are changed into his image. Our Transfiguration comes by him being transfigured before us. The Transfiguration of the Lord Jesus before us happens as we wait on him and look to him with an unveiled face.

Peter's reaction to this mountaintop scenario reveals something that is so common to the heart of man and yet so detrimental to our relationship with God. Rather than focus on the Lord, Peter focuses on two things that frequently distract God's people. These two things reveal Peter's desire to perform for God in order to get a specific result. Put another way, this is Peter's task-oriented response.

The first thing Peter fixates on is the place in which the experience is happening. Peter abruptly stands up, opens his mouth and says:

> **Lord, it is good for us to be here.**
>
> Matthew 17:4

Notice Peter says it is good for us to be **here**. Peter's first mistake is the same mistake that we almost all have the tendency to make and it is mishandling God's presence by attributing it to a place. He assumes that there is something spectacular about the location they are in. There is an amazing power encounter happening not ten feet away from Peter and he is fixating on what must make this place so special. He fails to realize that what makes the place special is not something inherently wonderful about the place; what is wonderful is the fact that Jesus is being manifested in his glory.

How many times, when a move of God begins to manifest, do we over emphasis the place over the person? How many times, when the Spirit of God begins to move, do we assume there must be something inherently wonderful about our leadership? How many times do we assume it's because we have paid a price, fasted enough, or somehow qualified to be having a move of God happening in our midst?

> *The more intimate we are with the Lord, the more revelation of him we carry.*

These thought processes are common to all of us. We all want to find a reason why God does what he does. And we like it even more if we feel we can say it's because of something we're doing; such as our fasting, our prayer groups, our teaching, etc. However, there wasn't anything magnificent about the mountain that caused Jesus to go there. The mountain was just a place Jesus could go to get away. What is magnificent is that Jesus is present and is revealing the tangible glory of God. God's presence moving in our midst is about heaven touching earth. When heaven touches earth, the earth begins to experience the power of the age to come. We must remember that God doesn't do wonderful things because we qualify or earn enough spiritual brownie points; he does wonderful things because he is wonderful.

The next thing Peter fixates on is the next logical step whenever the first mistake has been made. Peter's conclusion, to the fact that there must be something special about the location is:

> **...let us make here three tabernacles; one for thee, and one for Moses, and one for Elias.**
>
> Matthew 17:4

The purpose of the experience Jesus is having is relational and yet Peter is trying to launch the very first Christian building campaign. Being a part of what Jesus is building can certainly be very rewarding, however, there is a tendency in all of us to attempt to build that which God is not building. Peter's reaction, on top of this mountain, is very similar to another building program that was launched in the book of Genesis. At the Tower of Babel, "the people said to themselves "**let us build a tower which leads into heaven**." At that build site God scattered everyone into confusion.[3]

The response from heaven concerning these two issues in the heart of man is so poignant that God the Father felt it necessary to respond with a verbal rebuke. The response Almighty God gave to Peter was:

> **This is my beloved Son, in whom I am well pleased; hear ye him.**
>
> Matthew 17:5

---

[3] Joyner, Rick. There Were Two Trees in the Garden. Fort Mills : MorningStar Publications, 1985. p. 55. ISBN 978-1-929371-55-6; 1-929371-55-1.

If Peter had his way, that mountain would have likely become the Christian Mecca. You see, the Jews were looking for a savior to come who would be a great spiritual and political leader. They were looking for someone to come and rescue them from the tyranny of all that had been suffered. When Jesus came on the scene and explained that it was the kingdom of heaven that he was establishing, they had trouble understanding it. It is my opinion that Peter saw the situation happening in front of him and was looking for the initiation of a great takeover by the Lord. A takeover that would replace political leaders with spiritual leaders. A takeover that would start on that mountain. However, the purpose of the experience that Peter was having was simply to see and hear the Lord Jesus Christ as he truly is. This is where the Lord starts with all of us.

When God's presence is being manifested, it's so easy to want to build something. It is so easy to want to launch a campaign of some type. That need to "**build for ourselves a tower which leads into heaven**," is ingrained in the fallen nature of humanity and can only be broken by the power of the cross of Christ Jesus. How many revivals fall apart because of agendas and human needs to accomplish feats? There is nothing wrong with being a part of what Christ is building, but the reality is Christ is not building everything we say he is building. Sometimes he just wants us to enjoy his presence, but instead we try to launch a program.

Our purpose is to have relationship with the Lord Jesus Christ. Our goal is simply to know the Lord intimately. Before any project is begun, our first call is to come to the Lord Jesus, and see and hear him for who he is. Our first call is to come to the Lord and wait on him in his presence. It is the nearness of his presence or transfiguring glory that will change this world, not our personal objectives. Before we try to launch into personal kingdom building, we must remember the Lord's powerful remark, "This is my beloved son, in whom I am well pleased, listen to him." Focus on, surrender to, and be changed by him, then you will carry something that can touch the world.

Chapter 6
The Beloved

And Jesus, when he was baptized, went up straightway out of the water: and, lo, the heavens were opened unto him, and he saw the Spirit of God descending like a dove, and lighting upon him: And lo a voice from heaven, saying, This is my beloved Son, in whom I am well pleased.
Matthew 3:16-17

The very first announcement the Father made about his son Jesus was that he was beloved. When Jesus was baptized, he came up out of the water and the Father's voice rang out from heaven the words that "**this is my beloved son in whom I am well pleased**." This foundational statement about the Lord Jesus was so important that it warranted a manifestation of the audible voice of God to deliver. The Father could've said anything about the son and yet he chose this phrase. He could've said this is my son who will take away all your sin, but he didn't say that. The Father chose to make it crystal clear that the beloved nature of his son was important to him.

What most of us miss is that through the finished work of Jesus, we have been placed into Christ by the father. **Romans 8:1** tells us:

> ***There is* therefore now no condemnation to them which are (in Christ Jesus), who walk not after the flesh, but after the Spirit.**

Since the Father has placed every believer in Christ, everything that Jesus is due to inherit we are also due to inherit.

> **The eyes of your understanding being enlightened; that ye may know what is the hope of his calling, and what the riches of the glory of (his inheritance) in the saints, And what *is* the exceeding greatness of his power to us-ward who believe, according to the working of his mighty power…**
>
> Ephesians 1:18-19

This means that if the Father called Jesus the beloved, then every individual in Christ Jesus is the beloved one in whom God is well pleased. The Lord's pleasure rested on Jesus even though he had not done anything yet, and similarly his pleasure rests on us before we do anything "worthy" of being called the beloved.

A foundational revelation of Christ is that he is beloved, and so a foundational revelation of us is that we are the beloved. The meaning of the word "beloved" is defined using words such as loved, cherished, affectionately loved, adored and deeply loved. All of these words and more could be used to describe how God thinks, feels and acts towards us. If God feels this way towards us and it was important enough for him to audibly say it, then it must be foundational to our Christian lives to take on our identity as the beloved. Therefore, let us define ourselves as the beloved of God!

There are three primary things that cause a believer to act in opposition to their nature as the beloved. These three things are the lust of the eyes, the lust of the flesh, and the pride of life. We see these three things manifested in the temptations of Christ immediately following the Father's declaration that he was the beloved.

Immediately following the declaration from the Father that Jesus is the beloved, the Father lead Jesus into a place called the wilderness. The wilderness or "dark night of the wilderness," is a place that every believer must go sooner or later, and it is the place of the testing of the soul. It would seem that in order for us to walk in our nature as the beloved, God must take our relationship with him onto a battleground.

While each temptation of Jesus is a temptation to doubt his nature as the beloved, the first temptation is the lust of the flesh.

> **And when the tempter came to him, he said, If thou be the Son of God, command that these stones be made bread.**
>
> Matthew 4:3

Notice how the devil questions the nature of Christ and that he says, "if thou be the son of God." Likewise, in our relationship with God, the enemy comes to us and asks us the same question: "Are you really a son of God?" Then he starts by tempting our flesh. Commanding the stones to turn into bread is essentially the same thing as using the things of God to fulfill our own desires.

As I have mentioned before, there is a tendency in the fallen nature of man to use the things of God to feed our own desires. Of course, God is a good Father and he longs to bless us. Of course, God loves us and he wants to give us desires that he longs to fulfill. But there are desires within the carnal nature of man that lead us to use the things of God for our own benefit in such a way as to rob God of his glory. When a great evangelist, apostle, prophet or whatever, begins to receive God's hand of blessing, there is the soulish tendency to take that which God is revealing about himself and use it for their own benefit. When we do this, it just shows that we do not understand that we are the beloved. If we are resting in the arms of our Father as his beloved child, there really is no need to be sidetracked by lesser issues. We are the beloved and that is enough.

The next temptation that Christ suffered was the temptation to try to prove himself, the lust of the eyes.

> **Then the devil taketh him up into the holy city, and setteth him on a pinnacle of the temple, And saith unto him, If thou be the Son of God, cast thyself down: for it is written, He shall give his angels charge concerning thee: and in *their* hands they shall bear thee up, lest at any time thou dash thy foot against a stone.**
>
> Matthew 4:5-6

If the devil can get you defending yourself, then he knows he's gotten you out of Christ and out of your nature as the beloved. As I have mentioned, every believer is "in Christ," and Christ needs no defense. Because you have been put in Christ, when the devil tempts you to doubt you are the beloved, he is actually challenging Christ. This isn't to say that you cease to be you and become Christ, however, Christ is in you and you are in him.

To better understand the lust of the eyes and the tendency to try and prove yourself, we must first understand the nature of the eye. Jesus made it very clear to us that we must have purity of vision. Jesus said that "**if the eye is pure that the whole body will be full of light**." Part of the eye being pure is learning to have your vision focused on the Lord. When we are focused on the Lord, we won't try to prove ourselves. When we are focused on the Lord, we don't try to do things to exalt ourselves, we just try to exalt the Lord.

Jesus response to the devil's temptation was:

> **Jesus said unto him, It is written again, Thou shalt not tempt the Lord thy God.**
>
> Matthew 4:7

As we can see, the Lord's focus never wavered; it was always on the father and rooted in his identity as the beloved. Notice he referred to himself as God when he said, "**you shall not tempt the Lord thy God**." He never lost his focus; he functioned in the revelation of who he was. He was the beloved of the Father.

For you and me to keep from stumbling in this area called the lust of the eyes, we must revel in the truth that we are the beloved, while keeping our eyes focused on the Lord. If you think back over most of the sins you've fallen into, probably most of them occurred when you took your attention off the Lord for a minute and put it on something else. Most people don't intend to act against their nature as the beloved. However, when they remove their eyes from the Lord and put them on money, something like a Ponzi scheme can break out. When we take our eyes off the Lord for a minute and focus them on something like lust, then pornography and other sexual problems can arise. When we take our eyes off the Lord and focus them on a hurtful event someone inflicted on us, the results of that switching of focus can be anger, hatred, resentment, or bitterness. Jesus said the eye must be pure for the whole body to be full of light. Since we know this is true we can also infer that the opposite is true. If the eye is not pure the body may be filled with darkness. If darkness is in you how great is that darkness?

The way of the beloved is to keep our eyes on the Lord at all times. When our eyes shift focus it is then that we start to doubt the voice of God that speaks over us and says you're my beloved child in whom I am well pleased. The eye is the lamp of the body. Let's focus all of our conscious attention on the Lord and we will be full of light as God himself is light.

The way of the beloved is to keep our eyes on the Lord at all times.

The final temptation that Jesus endured, and all who are called the beloved must endure, is the boastful pride of life. Another way of saying this is taking short cuts to God's promise for us rather than following the Lord's leading.

> **Again, the devil taketh him up into an exceeding high mountain, and sheweth him all the kingdoms of the world, and the glory of them; And saith unto him, All these things will I give thee, if thou wilt fall down and worship me.**
>
> Matthew 4:89

Through the finished work of the cross, Jesus would inherit all the kingdoms of the world. The devil's temptation of the Lord is to take a quick route. Essentially, the devil is tempting the Lord Jesus to compromise in terms of his relationship with God in order to gain what God wanted to give to him, but gain it a wrong way.

God has a plan for our lives. Often times, the Lord will give us a glimpse of what is to come through our desires, our passions, and dreams. However, if we are not closely walking with God, we can end up leaping at opportunities that the Lord may not be giving us. These opportunities may seem ideal; these opportunities may seem like they are in fact God and turn out not to be from him at all.

The only way to keep from going the wrong route is to intimately know God. If we have a deep relationship with God, we won't be distracted by the things that present themselves as God but are not. How many ministers have a dream to do "great things for God." How many of them, in the process of trying to fulfill this dream, have gone out and taken a look at the kingdoms of this world and compromised on their relationship with God in order to gain the kingdom. In order to gain a following.

Jesus was never led by the carnal desire to gain the kingdoms of this earth. Jesus was led by his relationship with the Father. The Scriptures plainly tell us that Jesus said:

> **Then answered Jesus and said unto them, Verily, verily, I say unto you, The Son can do nothing of himself, but what he seeth the Father do: for what things soever he doeth, these also doeth the Son likewise.**
>
> John 5:19

Jesus did what he saw the Father doing. His relationship with the Father took priority in his life. Likewise, our relationship with the Father, the Son and the Holy Spirit must come first even above our calling. If this relationship does not come first, then sooner or later we will likely abandon it in order to "do" what we think we're supposed to do. In other words, if our relationship with God does not come first, we will end up grasping at things the Father wants to give us, but may be leading us away from because the source isn't Him.

How many times, in our attempt to get our ministries going, do we start trying to make something happen? In the day that we live in, it's so easy to want to market your ministry, market your book, market yourself on LinkedIn, Facebook or other avenues of media. It is possible to seek all of these things, thinking it is the will of God for us to do so, when in fact the Father may not be behind it. Yes, the Lord does open and shut doors for us. I am not saying you shouldn't use these avenues under the Lord's leadership. But we must be close to him in order to discern the nature of the door.

The most important thing in our lives is our relationship with God. And in all that we are and all that we do we must understand that God calls us the beloved. The beloved of God wants to rest in him, abide in him and know him. The beloved of God trusts God to lead them down the path. The beloved of God rests in the truth that God says, "You are my beloved child, in you I am well pleased." The beloved of God hears this voice in their heart and it is enough.

Chapter 7
Mary and Martha

But one thing is needful: and Mary hath chosen that good part, which shall not be taken away from her.
Luke 10:42

When the Israelites left Egypt, they were led by a cloud during the day and a fire during the night. Both the cloud and the fire were manifestations of God's presence. The Israelites simply followed the presence of God wherever he went. When the pillar moved they moved, and when the pillar stayed they stayed. No matter where they were or what condition they were in God provided for them and led them in the wilderness.

As ministers, it is our joy to become acquainted with the Lord's presence. When his presence is moving, we discern his moving and move with him. When his presence is resting, we discern his resting and rest with him. This is an adjustment from most people's normal way of life. Most people simply think in terms of doing whatever seems the most productive. However it is time we begin to look to the Lord and make it our goal to do whatever we see him doing just as he saw and did whatever he saw the Father doing.

Ministers are often sidetracked by the desire for results. Many times their leaders have asked them to be responsible for things and their thinking is that they are supposed to generate constant positive results. This causes them to try to make certain things happen and prevent others. This type of thinking isn't normal for those who are led by the spirit. Those who are led by the spirit are meant to do what they see the Father doing, while allowing the chips to fall where they may. Jesus went through periods of having large followings and he went through periods when those followings were scattered.

When we focus on activity rather than God, we can lose sight of what the Lord Jesus is saying and doing.

When we focus on activity rather than God, we can lose sight of what the Lord Jesus is saying and doing and begin the process of doing things for God, yet totally separate from him. Adopting this mindset means one may be generating a lot of "results" in ministry while others may simply be enjoying God's presence. The one who isn't generating results may actually be doing what God wants in that season.

There is a story in Luke 10, about two sisters named Mary and Martha. Jesus had come into a town to minister and while he was there, Mary and Martha were allowing him to stay with them. This likely meant that Jesus was using their house as a ministry base for people who wished to hear him speak.

As the story goes, Mary chose to sit at the feet of Jesus and listen to him speak. Martha, however, chose to be busy about the activities that needed to be done. Soon Martha had enough of it and decided that she was sick of doing all the things she was doing without any help and she went to Jesus and complained about her sister. Jesus response to Martha was that of a gentle rebuke. Jesus said:

> **Martha, Martha, thou art careful and troubled about many things: But one thing is needful: and Mary hath chosen that good part, which shall not be taken away from her.**
> Luke 10:41-42

This story reveals two different ways that many people choose to approach the Lord in life and ministry. The first way is through listening, stillness and resting in his presence. The second way is with activities, duties, and obligations that they feel are necessary. This is often rooted in a desire to stay in control so that "good things" can be assured of happening. Even more basic than this comes the understanding of being versus doing.

Martha represents those whose focus is on doing the work of the ministry, yet that work is not what God is currently doing. I look around today and I see so many people busy with work and things that they feel like they must do for God. We see this approach becoming more and more central to those in the body of Christ. It seems as though there is always a meeting to go to, a small group to attend or an event to volunteer for. I don't mean to suggest that doing things as the Lord leads you is bad or that people should sit around all day and do nothing. What I do mean to suggest is that there is a mindset that is becoming more popular today, and there is a risk within it that we can be led away from the Lord.

This destructive mindset that I speak of is taking our eyes off the Lord in favor of doing the things we think Jesus wants us to do. The very first revelation we have about Martha is that:

But Martha was cumbered about much serving.

Luke 10:40

It is interesting to note that serving was "cumbering" to her. It is also interesting to note that when it was time to focus on the Lord Jesus, Martha was off working. This is a common mistake that so many Christians are making today. The mistake I speak of is being away working when it is currently time for you to be in the presence of the Lord, hearing him speak. Many race off to work for God before He has truly been revealed to them. When this happens, the Christian work has actually become a distraction from the one the work is meant for. The point of our Christian lives is not to constantly be busy about the doing; it's about a relationship with the Lord Jesus himself.

The next thing that we hear coming out of the mouth of Martha is:

Lord, dost thou not care that my sister hath left me to serve alone?

Luke 10:40

Notice Martha's reaction to her frustration is to ask the question, "Lord, don't you care?" One way to see if you are in a Martha-style ministry is to ask yourself if you've been asking God this question. When things don't go quite like we would prefer or we're trying desperately to make some kind of mechanism work, it can be easy to want to ask God "don't you care?" The truth is, it wasn't that Christ did not care; it was that Christ was currently not doing what Martha was interested in doing. Martha was frustrated because she was trying to **make** something work. Martha's focus was out of season! Whenever our focus is on doing the things of the Lord rather than following the Lord we will frequently find ourselves floundering in frustration and wanting to ask God "why?" or "don't you care?"

This leads us to the next thing Martha said in her frustration:

> **...bid her therefore that she help me**.
>
> Luke 10:40

Another symptom that we have departed from our ministry of looking to the Lord Jesus in favor of being about the things of God is constant pleas for help with tasks. Martha's focus was not on what the Lord was saying and doing it was on what she was doing for the Lord. She was frustrated and went to the Lord and asked him to make her sister Mary help her. Likewise, when we are focused on what we are doing for God rather than simply first knowing him, we may go to God or people with constant pleas for help in our doing. How many times do we hear ministries constantly pleading for people's help? I'm not saying that it's bad to ask for help; I'm simply saying that if the pleas for help seem to outnumber the time spent with the Lord you likely have a problem somewhere.

After Martha finished speaking, the Lord Jesus spoke to her and began to address the root of her problem. The Lord's response was to tell Martha that her problem was in the area of anxiety. Jesus said to Martha:

> **Martha, Martha, thou art careful (Anxious) and troubled about many things:**
>
> Luke 10:41

How many times does anxiety over a task getting finished begin to surmount and we begin to lose our focus of the Lord Jesus? How many times do we as leaders require tasks be performed at the expense of people's spiritual life? How many times in the excitement of the doing do we lose the truth about the being (in his presence)? How many times, in the activity of the complex, do we forget that the Lord Jesus has simple tastes? Many people are haunted by the feeling that they must be busy about the work of the ministry in order for God to be happy with them and they end up missing God in the process.

Martha's response to this situation speaks to us. In the age of constant Bible studies, iPod preaching, small group ministries, and constant activity, Martha's activity speaks to us. Surely fellowship with other people is important. Surely we must not "forsake the gathering together of believers as is the habit of some." Surely the great commission is important. But we must keep our eyes on the Lord. History has shown, the vocation of minister has one of the highest burnout rates of any other vocation. And I believe it is time that we take an honest look at our lives and began to say to the Lord Jesus, "if my focus has gotten off of you and onto activity will you help me get my focus back on you?"

Jesus' praise of Mary reveals where he would prefer our focus be. Jesus said:

> **But one thing is needful: and Mary hath chosen that good part, which shall not be taken away from her.**
>
> Luke 10:42

His response shows us that he would prefer our attention to be on him rather than distracted by the doing. Some have said that there are people in this world who are *Marys* and there are people in this world who are *Marthas* and you can't really help which one you are. Still others have said that if the whole world was full of Marys then no Marthas would be getting anything done. I believe that being Mary or Martha is a choice, and sometimes we choose Martha because work is something we can control. When we choose Mary, we lose control to God, but the work we do is of a much higher order than before.

It is a hard choice to make intimacy with Jesus your focus. Learning how to wait at the feet of Jesus, listen to his voice and be intimate with him is a road many people do not take. However, this example reveals that it is the road we must take.

The Lord Jesus Christ is not an ethic, he is not a philosophy and he's not a set of rules and regulations to live by. The Lord Jesus Christ is a person and it takes time to get to know a person. It took time for me to know my wife the way I know her today. When I met her, I did not just walk up to her and ask her to marry me (although I thought about it). Jesus is the same. It is not a simple matter of sitting down, reading the Bible, going to Bible school, and all of a sudden, you're an authority of some kind. Jesus is all authority. Jesus is our Lord and he is our friend.

When you find yourself asking the question in your life and ministry, "God, don't you care I'm working and no one will help?" or "God, will you make them help me?", you need to remember the following:

"**Mary has chosen the better and it will not be taken away from her**."

We may be trying to remove from people the very thing the Lord wants them to have. It may be time to reset your focus. When we start with the being, the doing will come and it will come in a totally different way than us striving to make things happen.

Consider this parable for your mediation. A teacher asks a child to spend the weekend with two families. While the child visits with the first one, he sees a father spending the whole weekend desperately trying to get his son to understand math. When he visits the other, the father is a blind and deaf man who can only sit with his son gently in his lap. The child came back to the teacher and was asked, "Please tell me which one of the father's is blind." The child replied, "They both are, but only one can really see."

Chapter 8
Peace, Be Still

And he arose, and rebuked the wind, and said unto the sea,
Peace, be still. And the wind ceased,
and there was a great calm.
Mark 4:39

Much confusion exists over the issue of peace. Some people believe peace to be the absence of war or conflict. Some people believe peace to be a simple emotional feeling. Still, philosophers have meditated on peace for thousands of years and they have come up with partial truths, but not the whole truth.

One of the names of God used in the Scriptures is the name Jehovah Shalom. One of the first times this particular name for identifying God is used is in Judges 6. Many would recognize the story of Gideon and how God gave him such a supernatural victory over the Midianites. This story stands as one of the most prominent that we use to remind ourselves of God's ability in the face of uncertainty. It is a testimony to the fact that God can be trusted regardless of what we think or how we feel.

As the story goes, God appears to Gideon and tells him that he is going to use him to defeat the Midianites. At first, he is shocked, he makes comments about the fact that he doesn't know where God has been and how all of this has come to pass. However, the Lord makes it clear to Gideon that he will be with him. If you're not familiar with the story I would recommend reading it sometime, however, for the purposes of my teaching I will move on. The main point I want you to realize is that Gideon built an altar to the Lord and called that place Jehovah Shalom.

God can be trusted regardless of what we think or how we feel.

In order to correctly understand what a name of God says about his nature we have to understand a little bit about Jewish background. In Jewish culture, a person's name and their nature were very closely connected. For example, if someone was named Michael, and Michael means warrior, then it was believed that this person would become a warrior. Our society today does not operate this way. We tend to look at a list of baby names and then find the ones that sound the best to name our children. But Hebrew culture saw a direct correlation between a person's character and the name that they were given.

Understanding this about Jewish culture makes it easier to understand what is meant when God is identified by a specific name. Many have translated the name of Jehovah Shalom to mean God of Peace. However, it is more accurate to translate the name Jehovah Shalom as God *is* Peace. Not just God brings peace, not just God has peace or is capable of peace, God *is* peace. God himself literally is peace! Peace is not something that we have to beg God to give us; it is something he literally is. In other words, to grow in peace is to grow in God. To get more peace is to get more of God!

The closer we are in our relationship with God the more emotional peace we will experience. The truth is peace, like the presence of God, is something that we practice. We connect with God's peace as we practice his presence, stillness and rest. The closer we get to God the more his nature of peace will be attracted to us. As we learn to enter the deeper levels of intimacy with God, hidden things that prevent us from experiencing peace are removed and God's peace takes its place.

One of the best examples of the nature of peace is found in the story of Christ telling the storm to be still (Mark 4:39). As the story goes, Jesus along with the rest of his disciples, get in a boat to cross the sea of Galilee. While they are crossing, Jesus falls asleep below deck. While they are crossing, a storm comes up and these experienced fishermen thought they were going to die. During all of this, the Lord Jesus Christ remained asleep and only woke up when the disciples came to get him. When Jesus saw what was happening, he addressed the storm, spoke to it and said, "peace be still." When Jesus had done this, the storm subsided and he turned to the disciples and rebuked them for lack of faith.

There are some important principles the story reveals to us about the nature of peace and authority. Firstly, you only have authority over a particular area to the degree that you personally have victory in that area. What most people focus on is that Jesus stood up and said peace be still. It is no less miraculous that Jesus was sleeping in the midst of the storm. The spiritual principle is that Jesus walked in peace in the midst of all circumstances. Jesus relationship with the father secured him and gave him a sense of peace and rest that anchored his soul. Secondly, because Jesus had authority in the area of peace, he was able to release that peace outwardly. The same peace that allowed

Jesus to sleep in the middle of a storm gave him the authority to tell the storm to stop. This is the peace of God.

We have seen that one of the names of God is Peace, and Isaiah tells us the coming Messiah would be called Prince of Peace. We are also told that Jesus Christ is the exact representation of the Father (Hebrews 1:3). Jesus himself is peace.

As we learn to abide in Christ, we will grow in peace. Even if you're not sure it's happening at first, you will eventually notice a difference. As we grow in this authority of the peace of God, his peace will eventually be strong enough to reach out beyond us and touch the lives of those we come into contact with. Think about individuals that you get around and you just feel good in their presence. Now imagine that you're this person. When you learn to abide in Christ and rest in the presence of the Prince of Peace his peace will first settle things in your own life and then reach beyond you to touch those you come into contact with. The peace of Jesus calms every storm and removes every fear and does exactly for us as it did for the disciples on that boat, leaves us amazed.

Everything about the Lord Jesus is wonderful! And we are meant to constantly be growing in his presence, and his wonder. There's a Scripture in Proverbs that says:

> **But the path of the just *is* as the shining light, that shineth more and more unto the perfect day.**
>
> Proverbs 4:18

If our lives are not consistently growing in light and peace day by day, we need to ask God to shine his light on where we may have drifted off course. The

Christian life is meant to be getting better and better, not worse and worse. Granted, there may be seasons where it seems like things are getting worse because God is dealing with something, however, his hand is on us and we know in the midst of any chaos that he'll never leave us. I am not trying to say that if someone is struggling with a medical problem that God has left them, or that they've messed up too bad. However, I am saying that a symptom that we are growing in Christ Jesus is our ever-increasing peace and clarity.

Graham Cooke has often said that he doesn't allow his students to struggle with peace at the same level one year that they did the year before. If all of our lives were lived with a steady increase in the light and peace of God, the world would not be able to handle it. Wars would stop, gang members would go home, the anxious would be filled with God and the life of Christ would rule.

Come before the Lord Jesus Christ regularly, sit down before him and lean into his presence. Ask Jesus to come to you as the Prince of Peace and ask him to wash your mind in that peace. As you do, you'll sense the presence of our great Lord and Savior Jesus coming to you and saying, "Peace, be still."

Chapter 9
Profit and Loss

For whosoever will save his life shall lose it: and whosoever will lose his life for my sake shall find it. For what is a man profited, if he shall gain the whole world, and lose his own soul? or what shall a man give in exchange for his soul?
Matthew 16:25-26

In the Liam Neeson film version of *Les Miserables*, Neeson plays the main character, Jean Valjean. The movie opens with Valjean having just been released from prison. He is free to go look for work however, he has been given a passport that brands him a former criminal. As a result, Valjean is not able to find work and though he is technically free, he cannot fully embrace his freedom. It is as though he is still in prison.

One day Valjean finds himself face to face with a priest. Valjean is honest with the priest about his past and the fact that he is quite hungry and destitute. The priest invites him to stay the night in his lavish rectory and enjoy sleeping in a bed and eating a hot meal. During dinner, Valjean makes a sarcastic statement, saying that because of a meal and a bed that in the morning when he wakes up he will be a "new man."

In the middle of the night, the priest wakes up to the sound of rustling in the kitchen. When the priest goes into the kitchen, he sees Valjean stealing all of the silver and valuables he can. When the priest confronts Valjean, the former criminal hits the priest on the head and knocks him out. Valjean is then free to take off with all of the valuables.

In the morning, the priest is working in the rectory garden when the police bring in Jean Valjean. The police tell the priest that they have caught this criminal and that he has made an extraordinary claim. He claimed that all of the silver and precious items were a gift from the priest. When the priest hears this, he tells them, "Yes, I did." He then tells the police, "thank you for returning this man to me, he forgot the silver candle sticks." The priest then looks at Valjean and says, "Did you forget to take them?" The police leave and Valjean asks why the priest didn't turn him in. He responds by saying, "Don't ever forget that you've promised to become a new man." He continues saying, "Jean Valjean, my brother, you no longer belong to evil. With this silver, I've bought your soul and I've ransomed you back from fear and hatred. And I give you back to God."

The whole world seems to be full of people who wish to gain. People go to school to find out how they can get the best jobs and produce the most money. If they get the most money, they can afford the greatest luxuries such as expensive cars, bigger homes and all around comfortable living. The idea seems to be that anything that gets in the way of our gain is bad. If something seems to be hindering our hopes for gain, we do everything possible to remove that hindrance. It doesn't matter whether what we're trying to remove are people, friends, acquaintances or enemies. Generally speaking, we believe that gain is good and loss is bad.

This concept of gain being good and loss being bad is even seen some in Christianity. Some people believe that the larger organizational churches are obviously the ones that God is choosing to favor. The implication is that the smaller ones are not as favored. We even carry this gain attitude with us into our church life. Sometimes Christians step on the backs of other Christians in order to gain a seat of authority they feel due. Still others may gossip or manipulate situations in order to have leadership of a small group or some other church related activity. Don't get me wrong, I am not saying these types of issues are always the case, I am merely saying that life has programmed most of us to think a certain way and we tend to carry that into our Christian lives with others.

The problem with the gain approach to Christianity is that the kingdom of God operates on a different order than earthly kingdoms. The kingdom of heaven is not a right side up kingdom; it's an upside down kingdom.

> **But God hath chosen the foolish things of the world to confound the wise; and God hath chosen the weak things of the world to confound the things which are mighty**;
>
> 1 Corinthians 1:27

The kingdom of God isn't about becoming the highest leader it is about becoming the lowest servant.

> **And whosoever of you will be the chiefest, shall be servant of all**.
>
> Mark 10:44

In the kingdom of God, promotion means servanthood. I believe Jesus chose the example of a servant in his teachings to show that his kingdom would be of a different order than the "spiritual" kingdoms people had seen. Most people had seen the pharisaical approach to spirituality. This approach was one of a hierarchy of individuals. There were Chief Priests, regular Priests, Rabbis and so forth. Yet Jesus seems to make it clear that he does not want to re-create the systems of the world, which reach for the top. Jesus desire is to re-create the system of heaven, which touches the bottom.

While so many times we want to reach for those things which seem grandiose, the truth is that nothing is as grandiose as knowing the Lord Jesus Christ intimately. As a matter of fact, Paul said:

> **But what things were gain to me, those I counted loss for Christ. Yea doubtless, and I count all things *but* loss for the excellency of the knowledge of Christ Jesus my Lord**:
>
> Philippians 3:7-8

When Paul made this statement, he had just talked about the great zeal with which he religiously performed tasks. Paul was an incredibly qualified religious person. Paul was trained by a man named Gamaliel, one of the greatest teachers/philosophers of that time. Paul religiously persecuted Christians because he felt that he was doing the will of God by killing them. His performance pushed him to do the unthinkable. In today's terminology, Paul was as bad as a terrorist. Similarly, there are times that we reach for this grandiose status that Paul had and it pushes us to a place we don't need to go: away from the presence of the Lord.

It could be said that dead religion is self-aggrandizing. When we curry for points with the pastor so that he will listen to our teachings and promote us with the people, we are self-aggrandizing. When we see another ministry's success as a threat to us and we begin to subtly put them down and elevate ourselves, we become self-aggrandizing.- If we promote our gifts so that people will listen to us rather than promoting the Lord who gave the gifts, we are self-aggrandizing. All of which is the exact opposite of Paul's commission to take everything that could be counted as gain; pride, money, religious status, and count it all as lost for the sake of knowing Jesus. In the upside down kingdom that we live in, you can gain everything and you find that you lost everything on the way. However, you can lose everything and find that you've gained everything.

The follower of Christ Jesus doesn't seek gain but loss. I don't mean to suggest that all gain is bad. We have to make a living and support our family. The loss I mean is seeking the kingdom of God First. "**Seek first the kingdom of God and all of these things shall be added unto you.**" If we lose our jobs for choosing to follow Christ Jesus, our loss in the world becomes a gain in the kingdom. If we choose to forgo building a financial empire in order to first build the kingdom of God, our loss becomes gain. If we choose not to treat people as inferior to us, but as equals with us needing Jesus, our loss of superiority becomes gain. If we lose our immediate ministry because the Lord says it's time for another ministry to rise up (such as the case with John the Baptist), the kingdom of God is advanced and loss is turned into gain. If we spend our whole lives praying for another person's success and yet no one ever knows what we do in secret, loss is turned into gain.

The kingdom that we walk-in has some tricky roads to navigate. As I've said, you can gain everything only to find that you've lost everything. You can also lose everything to find that you gained everything. The kingdom of God is not meant to be filled with religious snobbery, but rather selfless camaraderie. Brothers who are more like David than like Saul. Brothers who see the kingdom they are entrusted with as belonging to God while they are just stewards following his lead.

The kingdom of God is meant to lead every believer down a wondrous path of gain. The starting point of this path is laying everything down, but what we pick up is grander than any of us can imagine when we first began. At first, this seems fearful to let go of that which we want to hang onto. After we let go we realize that a new freedom has emerged and our loss has turned into a great gain. In the gain that we attain we find some of the wonders that God has for us. In the gain that we walk in, we find ourselves living as those who have nothing and yet possess all things. For what does it profit a man to gain the whole world, but to lose his own soul? Understand this great wisdom of Christ and you will understand the revelation of profit and loss.

Chapter 10
Go and Sin No More

And Jesus said unto her, Neither do I condemn thee: go, and sin no more.
John 8:11

Every year, there's a major event that takes place in the south. During this event businesses close, weddings aren't scheduled and some funerals are even delayed. It's like a regional holiday on one particular Saturday in the fall. The day I speak of is the day the University of Alabama plays Auburn University in football. It is called the Iron Bowl. The game is usually a good one. When these two teams play each other, regardless of what the season has looked like, the gloves come off and the focus is on. Fans all say that they want to beat the other team bad or "shut them out," but I think deep down most people are really hoping for a close game. They want the game to be really close and then at the last minute have their team win. How does one win at football? Simply put, one teams score is higher than the other when time runs out. But have you ever wondered what football would look like if no one was keeping score?

To put it simply, you only get to win at something when you choose to keep score. If you don't keep score it just becomes a bunch of people hanging out on a field throwing a ball back and forth. If you don't keep score the point of it all begins to drift away and the hook in people's attention begins to drop. Similarly, many people are trying to keep tabs on how they're doing spiritually. I call this an attempt to micromanage their own spirituality. In a sense, they are trying to apply a worldly thought process to a spiritual concept. They are trying to win at spirituality. This usually leaves them highly frustrated and feeling like they can't get anywhere in terms of their relationship with God. The truth of the matter is it's not up to us to keep score on our spirituality because Christ has already won the game.

John 8 tells the story of a woman who was caught in the act of adultery. She is discovered in the very act of her sexual sin and the scribes and Pharisees bring her before Jesus to see what he would say about it. The motivation of the scribes and Pharisees was to trap the Lord in some way, but that did not happen. The woman is brought before Christ and the Pharisees accuse her to Jesus. While this is taking place, Jesus stoops down and begins writing on the ground. The scribes and Pharisees continue to press Jesus for a response and Jesus stands up and says, "Let he who is without sin cast the first stone." The moment Jesus says this, he stoops back down and begins writing in the dirt once again. And the scribes and Pharisees are so convicted that they left, starting with the oldest and ending with the youngest. When they had all left, Jesus stood up and looked at the woman and said, "Woman, where are your accusers?" She responds by answering him and saying that no one was accusing her. Jesus replies, "Then neither do I condemn you, go and sin no more."

This story is an example of the grace and love of Jesus for everyone. The examples in it show us that God is loving and that our sins can't keep us from him. Of course, sin is not something we want to do or not deal with if it's in our lives. However, this story reveals the love and grace of Jesus and how he treats the sin issues that come up in our life. To better understand this let's take the story apart and work through it a little bit.

The story begins with the scribes and the Pharisees bringing the woman who had committed sexual sin to Jesus.

> **And the scribes and Pharisees brought unto him a woman taken in adultery;**
>
> John 8:3

The Pharisees were a religious order that paid meticulous attention to the law to try and keep from sinning. Their focus was on the black and white issues of the law and they really didn't see anything between those two issues. The scribes were an order that kept records and wrote official documents in certain settings. So what we have is those who see things as a black and white matter of the law, mixing with those who keep records of events coming together to form an accusation against this woman.

> **They say unto him, Master, this woman was taken in adultery, in the very act. Now Moses in the law commanded us, that such should be stoned: but what sayest thou?**
>
> John 8:4-5

The combination of these two ideas is what forms most accusations. First, the enemy accuses you based on what you've done wrong and then reminds you of all the times you've done wrong. I like to refer to this as the inner Pharisee. Everyone has an inner Pharisee that needs to meet the grace of God. If it hasn't met the grace of God it will continue to partner with the enemy to receive accusations against you. This is not what the Lord wants for us!

The key to a breakthrough of the love and grace of Jesus is to pay careful attention to Christ's response to the situation.

> **But Jesus stooped down, and with *his* finger wrote on the ground, *as though he heard them not*.**
>
> John 8:6

Similar to how Christ stooped down and began to write in the dirt, the Lord came down from heaven in order to touch the earth on our behalf. The Scriptures tell us that all of us are made from the dirt.

> **And the LORD God formed man *of* the dust of the ground, and breathed into his nostrils the breath of life; and man became a living soul.**
>
> Genesis 2:7

Just as Jesus wrote on the ground, he desires to take his finger and write his story in all of our lives. No matter what condition our life is in, the Lord desires to take our mess and turn it into something wonderful. This is the grace of God!

When the scribes and Pharisees pressed Jesus for an answer, he gave a response meant to destroy the accusation.

> **So when they continued asking him, he lifted up himself, and said unto them, He that is without sin among you, let him first cast a stone at her. And again he stooped down, and wrote on the ground.**
>
> John 8:7-8

The scribes and Pharisees felt that they could accuse her because they were keeping score. However, Jesus response was to show them that if they were going to judge people by keeping score, then they would have to see that they had points on the board as well. Just like all of us, there is no one that doesn't have bad points on that particular scoreboard.

Jesus ultimately breaks the scoreboard over this lady when he responds to her specifically.

> **When Jesus had lifted up himself, and saw none but the woman, he said unto her, Woman, where are those thine accusers? hath no man condemned thee? She said, No man, Lord. And Jesus said unto her, Neither do I condemn thee: go, and sin no more**.
>
> John 8:10-11

When Jesus saw no one but the woman, he was finally in the position to speak directly to her as one representing the Father. Then Jesus reveals the scandal of grace, he tells her that he does not condemn her and that she may go free and sin no more. Looking at this situation the way the scribes and Pharisees did, this woman had in fact sinned and deserved the stoning she was about to receive. However, Jesus reveals that he is no longer keeping score. When Jesus went to the cross, he took the score and the scoreboard with him and they were both nailed to the tree. Jesus looked at this woman and said to her that he wasn't keeping a record but it's time to be free. Sin puts people into bondage and because of the bondage it creates, the Lord does not want us under its hold. The Lord's response is simple, "you are not condemned, but it's time to be free."

We only live in shame and accusation when we believe that God is still keeping score. The reason we believe he is keeping score is because it is us that's doing the scorekeeping. We make the mistake of judging God as being just like us. We forget the words of Blaise Pascal who said, "God created man in his own image and man returned the compliment." Just like the football analogy I gave earlier, we all like to know what the score is because it gives us a false sense of control, a sense of how our spirituality is doing. The truth is that it is Christ who is in control now. Until we let go, until we surrender our whole lives to Christ and stop micromanaging our spirituality, we'll never be fully free from the sense of shame and accusation that has already been dealt with at the cross.

Jesus went to the cross despising the shame. All of it was placed on Jesus and as such we receive his life as our own. One of my favorite quotes is by Thomas Merton who said, "Quit keeping score altogether and surrender yourself with all your sinfulness to God who sees neither the score nor the score keeper but only his child redeemed by Christ."[4] The answer to everything, the way to freedom is the cross of Jesus. Through the power of the cross of Jesus, we are redeemed and the score and the actions of the scorekeeper (the inner Pharisee) are all settled in him.

---

[4] Merton, Thomas. quoted by Brennan Manning, The Rabbi's Heartbeat. Colorado Springs : NAVPRESS, 2003. p. 13. ISBN I-57683-469-7.

Chapter 11
The Spirit of Prophecy

...for the testimony of Jesus is the spirit of prophecy.
Rev 19:10

What does it mean to really know someone? Does it mean that you experience closeness with them that you do not have with everyone else? Does it mean that you are experienced enough with their actions that you have a good chance of being able to guess what they will do in a given circumstance? A lot of questions must be asked in terms of coming to know someone and what that means. However, most people would agree that to really know someone you have to spend time with them and through personal experience come to know what they are like.

To know what someone is like you have to be willing to understand who they really are and not just certain details about them that you perceive through your own prejudices. For example, when a new married couple has been together for several months they often go through a phase where one spouse does something and the other spouse judges what they are doing based off their perception of what they meant when they did it. One of the most difficult lessons to learn in marriage is that your perception of what someone means can be totally different than what they actually meant. Once this lesson is learned understanding can began to unfold between spouses and healing can emerge.

Similarly to the spouses relationship to the other spouse, we have to come to know the Lord Jesus Christ as he is. Coming to know the Lord Jesus is a process that takes place over time. Between us and the Lord there are veils that have to be removed so that we are able to see Jesus as he is:

> **Nevertheless when it shall turn to the Lord, the vail shall be taken away**.
>
> 2 Corinthians 3:16

As we surrender to the Lord Jesus and turn to him, the veils between us and him are taken away and a revelation of who Christ is begins to emerge. Consequently, the deeper the intimacy we have with Jesus, the deeper the revelation of who Jesus is we will carry.

As Jesus is revealed to us, we behold his image and are changed into the likeness of what we see:

> **But we all, with open face beholding as in a glass the glory of the Lord, are changed into the same image from glory to glory, *even* as by the Spirit of the Lord.**
>
> 2 Corinthians 3:18

The previous Scripture refers to beholding the Lord as in a glass (mirror), and being changed into the image of what we see. This is saying that as we see Christ the way he is, a mirror image of him is formed within us. This is how we are formed into the same image and likeness of Jesus, by "looking unto Jesus the author and finisher of our faith." This formation of Christ Jesus within us is also the operation of something called the spirit of prophecy.

Revelation 19:10 says, "The testimony of Jesus is the spirit of prophecy." In other words, the testimony or understanding of the nature of Jesus fits into the order of what is called prophecy. A true revelation of prophecy always reveals the nature of Jesus Christ, if it does not it cannot be said to be of the nature of the spirit of prophecy. I have often had conversations with individuals who desire to become more "prophetic." They ask me what they should do or what they should pray in order to see the prophetic released in their lives to a higher degree. My response to them is always the same; if you desire to be prophetic you must meditate the Gospels and allow the testimony or revelation of who Jesus is to be built into you. This is done by meditating the Scriptures and learning to abide in the presence of the Holy Spirit.

One example of the spirit of prophecy is found in Matthew 16. Jesus is talking with his disciples and he asks each of them, "Who do men say that I am?" There is a discussion amongst the disciples concerning what people believe about Jesus, however none of them are quite right. Then Jesus asked the question, "Who do you say that I am?" Once the question is asked, Peter says, "You are the Christ, the son of the living God." Notice that Peter revealed an accurate testimony of who Jesus is. It is interesting to see that immediately following this accurate testimony of Jesus, the Lord immediately begins to prophesy to Peter saying:

> **Blessed art thou, Simon Barjona: for flesh and blood hath not revealed *it* unto thee, but my Father which is in heaven. And I say also unto thee, That thou art Peter, and upon this rock I will build my church; and the gates of hell shall not prevail against it. And I will give unto thee the keys of the kingdom of heaven: and whatsoever thou shalt bind on earth shall be bound in heaven: and whatsoever thou shalt loose on earth shall be loosed in heaven.**
>
> Matthew 16: 17-19

It's almost like Jesus can't help himself, the testimony has come forth and the natural progression of the testimony is the prophetic.

Implied within this teaching on the spirit of prophecy, is the notion that how you perceive the Lord will affect your ministry to individuals. If you believe Jesus is love and therefore utterly loving, you will portray him as such to those you minister to. If you believe that Jesus is angry, you will portray Christ with an angry edge. Essentially, our misperception about Jesus as being angry will cause us to lead others to believe that Jesus is angry. If we believe that Jesus is mostly forgiving, but holds a little bit against us, we will communicate Jesus as if he was somewhat divided in his mindsets. The point that I'm making is clear, how we see Christ effects how we minister in the world. The reason, the spirit of prophecy.

Having an accurate testimony of Jesus is of supreme importance to all of us. We must know that he is love. We must know that he is light. We must know that he is peace. We must know that God is our shield and our exceedingly great Lord. We must know that the

Lord is our leader, our shepherd, our defender, our healer, our Savior and our provider. We must have this revelation of Christ so formed within us that we accurately portray him to those we minister to.

Having an inaccurate perception of Christ has had grave consequences to us in the world today. When Jesus asked, “Who do men say that I am?” the answers the disciples gave were false. How many false or distorted understandings of Jesus are in the world today? I confess that when we make mistakes in our ministries, those mistakes made on details or unintentional slips of facts seldom bother me. What I find a lot of danger in is when I see people ministering who are making mistakes that show they have an obvious image of God problem. If you prophesy that God’s going to do something in three years and he ends up doing it in five years, that is not missing it in the spirit of prophecy. What is missing it in the spirit of prophecy is portraying Jesus in a way that he is not such as angry, judgmental or condemning.

The consequences of having an inaccurate perception of Jesus are clearly visible in the world today. What this world needs is a true revelation of the Christ. Seeing the Lord Jesus Christ is accomplished through intimacy. Seeing the Lord Jesus is accomplished by the spirit of wisdom and revelation mentioned in Ephesians 1:17-18. Seeing the Lord Jesus Christ is accomplished as we meditate on him, look to him and spend time under the shadow of his gaze. As we rest in the Lord Jesus Christ, we are changed into the same image we see from glory to glory. An accurate testimony of Jesus is formed in us and our ministry to others becomes more and more true.

Come to the Lord Jesus. Ask him to reveal himself to you as he is. Spend some time meditating some of the stories in the Gospels and asking the Holy Spirit to reveal the Lord Jesus Christ to you. It is good, it is necessary and it is what is most needed today. We will only be kind to the degree that we experience his kindness. We will only be loving to others to the degree that we experience his love. The testimony of Jesus Christ really is prophetic and it begins in us by learning to abide in the presence of the Lord.

Chapter 12
Baptism and Abiding in Union

It is expedient for you that I go away: for if I go not away, the Comforter will not come unto you.
John 16:7

The first baptism we experience is the baptism in water. This is being baptized into Christ's death.

Know ye not, that so many of us as were baptized into Jesus Christ were baptized into his death?

Romans 6:3

Through this our old man dies to the world which makes us in the world but not of it. It is also where we receive newness of life and are positioned in Christ's resurrection.

For if we have been planted together in the likeness of his death, we shall be also *in the likeness* of *his* resurrection:

Romans 6:5

The second baptism we experience is the baptism of the Holy Spirit. In this we are baptized into the Lord's presence. The Holy Spirit is the "**spirit of life**," (Romans 8:2) when his presence comes, he fuses us with his life. This baptism launches us into intimacy with Jesus and establishes us in his victory.

I have talked about coming before the Lord to wait in his presence. So the first thing we are waiting on is the promise the Lord Jesus gave to his disciples. Jesus told his disciples to go and to wait for the promise of the Holy Spirit.

> **And, behold, I send the promise of my Father upon you: but tarry ye in the city of Jerusalem, until ye be endued with power from on high**.
>
> Luke 24:49

When Jesus walked this earth, he talked of the necessity that he leave the earth. The necessity that he leave was so that the Holy Spirit may come. He said, "**Unless I go the helper cannot come**." (John 16:7) Jesus told us that when he left, his spirit, the spirit of Christ would come. This coming meant the Holy Spirit will forever dwell within us.

When Jesus spoke to his disciples, he told them the Holy Spirit "**is with you and shall be in you**." (John 14:17) The Lord Jesus breathed on them after his resurrection and said, "**receive the Holy Spirit**" and then he told them to go and wait for the coming of the Holy Spirit. Interesting, did the Holy Spirit come and then leave. No, the Holy Spirit was with the disciples but was preparing to come in and abide in the disciples.

My own experience of being filled with the Holy Spirit began my first year of college. I was in the midst of an extraordinary trial, although I've had trials since that made this one look like nothing. There is nothing like having life fall apart to get you seeking the Lord. I received the Lord Jesus as my Savior during this trial, but I began to realize that my current experience of God wasn't strong enough to see me through the ordeal I was in. I knew Jesus as my savior but I didn't know him as a friend who sticks closer than a brother. As the fullness of what I was going through began to unfold, I began to have an ache for the Lord to touch the deepest places of my heart. As I pored through the scriptures and purchased countless teachings from Christian leaders and authors, I began to be aware that there was something called the baptism of the Holy Spirit. The more I learned, the more I understood that this was something of a hot topic in Christian circles. I had attended a conservative church for many years and I found out that if I brought up the baptism of the Holy Spirit with my friends, they looked at me like I was nuts.

The more I sought God, I realized that this encounter with the fullness of the Holy Spirit was what I needed. Everyone I found who had been baptized in the Holy Spirit seemed to have a well of life flowing from deep within them. So I did the only thing I knew to do, I wrote a letter to a popular ministry who taught on the baptism of the Holy Spirit. A few weeks went by and I received a letter in the mail from this ministry. I opened the letter and when I read it, it was like a light came on and I knew life was about to change. The letter instructed me to simply come before the Lord Jesus (the baptizer), ask him to fill me with his spirit, yield completely to him (including my mouth) and wait. Just like Jesus' instruction to the disciples to wait on the promise, I was to do the same.

That night I came before the Lord and did as the letter instructed. Some time went by and I fell asleep while waiting. Suddenly! Without warning, the Holy Spirit fell on me with tremendous power. I immediately began speaking in a language that I did not know and I felt as though my heart was being touched with the purest love I had ever encountered. As I sat in the presence of the Lord, I knew that I was encountering the living God and that nothing in my life would ever be the same. I began to see visions of the God of the Ancients or The Ancient of Days. The only question I could think of was, God, who are you?

It has been my experience that the greater we surrender to the Lord, the greater the filling of his presence. The more we surrender our hopes, our dreams, our fears, the more he can move within us. The filling with Holy Spirit is one of the initial encounters that God has for all believers. It doesn't mean that before it happens you don't have the Holy Spirit. It does mean that when it does happen the Holy Spirit has more of you.

When God's presence touches you in the deepest places of your heart, nothing is ever the same. Nothing will ever satisfy you but getting closer and closer to Jesus. The way has been opened for all believers to enter into an adventure with God. This adventure starts with his presence and as the Lord reveals himself to us, we continue to become better acquainted with the Most High God. His presence opens the door for abiding in union with Jesus.

The baptism is for all believers, but unfortunately many believers stop here. They never go on in their relational experience of Jesus. The life we live is one where we learn to abide in the resurrected Christ. We really have been given a new life.

If you've never received the fullness of the Holy Spirit in your life, it's time to ask Him to come. Jesus is the baptizer and all you need to do is ask him to send the Holy Spirit. Find a quiet place and completely yield to the Holy Spirit. Yield everything including your mouth to the Holy Spirit. Focus all your attention on his loving presence and ask Jesus to send the Holy Spirit to fill you. Wait expectantly and he will come. Sometimes it takes people a while to fully surrender, but when you receive the Holy Spirit as a gift, he will come.

Chapter 13
Love

A new commandment I give unto you, That ye love one another; as I have loved you, that ye also love one another.
John 13:34

Have you ever tried to command someone to love you? If you have, you probably found out pretty quick that love just doesn't work like that. If you've never tried it and you feel like giving it a shot, go for it and see what kind of response you get. Most likely, it will involve the police department, a helmet or contact gear of some kind. Love is not something that can be forced, it is something that is.

If you really think about Jesus' command that we love each other, you might find yourself face-to-face with the reality that you are in no way equipped to answer this command. You might find yourself thinking, how am I supposed to love everyone? On my best days I struggle loving the people closest to me. When we look at ourselves and attempt to do something by our own ability, we will always be left feeling frustrated because we're measuring a situation by our ability.

However, Jesus command that we love one another isn't meant to frustrate us it is meant to reveal the nature of God. God never asks us to do anything that doesn't originate with Him. In fact, when God asks us to do something it is a sure sign that he has already begun to move in our lives in that area.

> **Or who hath first given to him, and it shall be recompensed unto him again? For of him, and through him, and to him, *are* all things: to whom *be* glory for ever. Amen.**
>
> Romans 11:35-36

Therefore, when we are instructed to love others, it does not mean that we must try in our flesh to love; it means that the Lord intends to do the loving for us. It also means that the Lord first intends to love us.

In any area of our lives where we do not experience the love of Christ Jesus we will be limited in our ability to love others. In the discussion of love, most people feel they aren't completely loved by the Lord Jesus Christ. Whenever this is the case, it will usually be manifested in some way in our lives: anger, irritability, sadness, etc. Thus limiting our ability to love others. When these things are present it is frequently a sign that the love of God has not been made perfect in us.

> **He that feareth is not made perfect in love.**
>
> 1 John 4:18b

Another way of saying this is that the presence of emotions which create an inner sense of instability is a sign that something is blocking the love of God in our lives.

By and large, the number one feeling people have that seems to block their sense of the love of God is the belief that God is mad at them. In all of the counseling and ministry I've done, I have to say that this notion is one of the more common that I run into. Generally, people feel that they have made some mistakes along the way or perhaps a series of mistakes and this puts them on God's anger list. Whenever this happens, I first make sure the individual understands the nature of God's anger.

It is scary to think about wrath coming from God. Most people read scriptures in the Bible that seem to present God's anger and they wonder if it's possible God could feel that way with them. What they assume is that there is something in them that God is mad at and he might pour his wrath out on them. In a sense this is true but in the way that we normally think of wrath it actually isn't.

Wrath is not something that is poured out against an individual because they screw up, wrath is a mechanism that God uses to remove sin.

> **For the wrath of God is revealed from heaven against all ungodliness and unrighteousness of men, who hold the truth in unrighteousness.**
>
> Romans 1:18

Notice that the Scripture above says that wrath is being revealed against the ungodliness and unrighteousness "of" men. Most people read the Scripture above and think that it is saying God is pouring out wrath against ungodly and unrighteous men; this is not what the Scripture says here. Wrath is what God pours out against sin in order to remove it. Put another way, sin is what harms us, and so the Lord uses something called wrath in order to remove what is harming us. Often times we feel the intensity of this wrath and internalize it as something that's coming against our personhood when the reality is it is coming against the thing that is hurting us… Sin.

The reason wrath can come against the sins committed by the person rather than the person doing the sin is because of the finished work of the cross. When Jesus Christ went to the cross, all of the individual sins as well as sin as a principal were laid on Jesus.

> **For he hath made him *to be* sin for us, who knew no sin; that we might be made the righteousness of God in him.**
>
> 2 Corinthians 5:21

Since sin was put on Jesus, when he went to the cross the wrath of God that was poured out on Jesus was being poured out against sin. When Jesus was in the garden of Gethsemane, he made the statement:

> **Father, if thou be willing, remove this cup from me.**
>
> Luke 22:42

The Book of Revelation talks about cups or bowls that are filled with wrath. Jesus knew when he went to the cross, wrath was going to be poured out against all of the power of sin that had been laid on Jesus. Jesus act on the cross during those hours in which he was in excruciating pain was to allow the work of wrath to fully consume the power of all of the sin that had been put on him. When Jesus declared "**it is finished**," the work of God's wrath consuming sin in Christ had been completed. Once Jesus work was completed, he surrendered to the father and when he died, the power of sin died in Christ.

Now that we have seen that wrath is what God uses to destroy sin, we can see wrath for what it is... A manifestation of the love of God. Wow! That's different than what most people think! When God begins to pour out his wrath on sin, it is a manifestation of his love whereby he becomes a little bit more intentional about freeing you from what is killing you. The effect of sin is what kills people spiritually. When God pours out his wrath on you it isn't because his hatred is burning towards you, it is because he hates what is harming his child. If you saw your child being harmed, would you not run as fast as you possibly could and stand between your child and danger?[5]

The Scriptures talk about love casting out fear because fear has torment.

> **There is no fear in love; but perfect love casteth out fear: because fear hath torment. He that feareth is not made perfect in love.**
>
> 1 John 4:18

The reason fear has torment is because fear is produced by the perception of being blocked from the love of God. Through the finished work at the cross, you are no longer blocked from the love of God by anything. Our being allowed to embrace that we are 100% loved by God with nothing blocking the way is what opens the door for us to receive the love of God in our life. Jesus work on the cross reconciled us to him.

---

[5] Jacobsen, Wayne. He Loves Me! Second. Newbury Park : Windblown Media, 2007. pp. 118-123. ISBN 978-0-9647292-5-4.

To wit, that God was in Christ, reconciling the world unto himself, not imputing their trespasses unto them; and hath committed unto us the word of reconciliation.

2 Corinthians 5:19

Everyone on this planet exists in the state of being what we call "reconciled to God." Does this mean that everyone on earth is saved and going to heaven? No... Salvation comes through faith and relationship with Jesus Christ, the Father and the Holy Spirit. However, everyone is reconciled to God and through Jesus Christ, the love of God is fully realized.

There is no amount of evil that you can do that can prevent God from loving you. There is no one that you could murder, no one that you could steal from and no one that you can hurt that could change the way God thinks and feels about you. God's love for you is perfect and as you are fully reconciled to your reconciliation in Christ, your love for others is perfected. If there is anything in your heart that you believe you have done that has blocked your sense of God's love for you, hand it over to Jesus now... Let him take it and lift it out of your heart... He loves you and he is calling to you to receive his love and go forth into the world in the light of his love and share it with everyone you come across.

Chapter 14
Spiritual Authority

For verily I say unto you, That whosoever shall say unto this mountain, Be thou removed, and be thou cast into the sea; and shall not doubt in his heart, but shall believe that those things which he saith shall come to pass; he shall have whatsoever he saith.
Mark 11:23

One of the most needed elements in our Christian lives is the element of spiritual authority. Spiritual Authority is what enables us to look at the dead and say they are only asleep. Spiritual authority is what enables us to look at the lame and say get up pick up your mat and walk. It gives us the authority to call out the scribes and say woe unto you. And it gives us the ability to walk straight into a squall line and say stop, peace, be still. It enables us to look at the demonized and say be delivered. It makes it so that we can walk down the street and find that people are recovering all around us because our shadow has fallen on them.

Spiritual authority is one of the most misunderstood elements of our spiritual lives. Many times we think we know who's operating in it and then we come to find out we were completely mistaken. We may assume that a "spiritual leader," has spiritual authority while a janitor doesn't, only to find out that in that particular instance the opposite was true. Spiritual authority is often assumed to be directly linked with leadership, platform or visibility of some kind. However, we learn from Saul and David that this situation is not always the case. You see, Saul was king and David was not and yet David had spiritual authority and Saul did not. Spiritual authority is of a completely separate order than natural authority.

All authority is allowed by God and therefore must be honored.

> **Let every soul be subject unto the higher powers. For there is no power but of God: the powers that be are ordained of God.**
>
> Romans 13.1

However, not all authority is spiritual and of the order of heaven. In Matthew 28, Jesus lists two places authority exists, Heaven and Earth. Civil authorities are allowed by God and where there is no biblical discrepancy they must be followed. However, there is an order that is higher than civil, that which is spiritual and on these matters **we ought to obey God rather than men.** (Acts 5:29) It is the discrepancy between the natural and the spiritual that has caused great harm in this matter.

One of the worst deceptions that "religious leaders" have taught is that spiritual authority and natural authority are always linked together automatically. The 1970s saw a movement which has become known as the "shepherding movement." The deceptions and distortions taught throughout this movement were of diabolical proportions. Followers were taught to listen to leaders with no questions asked. Children who had heard from the Lord to do something (go into missions, feed the hungry, etc.) were told that if their parents said no it was better that they obey their parents rather than God. This is a major distortion seeing how when Jesus left his family to go minister as a child, they rebuked him but he said, **How is it that ye sought me? wist ye not that I must be about my Father's business?** (Luke 2:49) Spiritual authority and natural authority are not linked automatically. If they were, Jesus would have submitted to the Pharisees.

The danger of false teachings on authority has caused people to fear man rather than God. When leadership demands unwavering loyalty of its people, it generally ends up spiritually castrating them so that they can't hear the voice of God. In many cases, when the views of authority have become "religious," the leadership goes on to accuse its followers for not being proactive about their spirituality. Interesting, this form of leadership wants you to obey man rather than God and then judges the people for the results it brings.

In all things, we need balance and I want to make sure there is a balance to this teaching. Many people who would take what I am sharing and use it to try to excuse rebellion. This is not my goal. My goal is not to get you into an opinion war with your pastor. My goal is not to puff you up in your thinking so that you begin moving in an illegitimate spirit. My goal isn't to tell you to resist a leader in their sphere of authority because you feel you know what God wants. My goal is to open the way to spiritual authority by pointing to the one who has it.

We only come to operate in spiritual authority by relationship with its author. People may promote us, leaders may maneuver themselves politically and leadership may rise up, which is all allowed by God. However, though a pastor, apostle or some other spiritual leader is promoted, it does not mean that they are operating in spiritual authority automatically.

Concerning spiritual authority Jesus made the statement:

> **All power (authority) is given unto me in heaven and in earth**.
>
> Matthew 28:18

Since all authority is given to Jesus, it is only received by learning to abide in him. Spiritual authority is part of our bearing fruit:

> **Abide in me, and I in you. As the branch cannot bear fruit of itself, except it abide in the vine; no more can ye, except ye abide in me**.
>
> John 15:4

So, learning to abide in Jesus is where the authority to move mountains comes from. As we abide in him, our lives begin to bear fruit and that fruit is for the Lord.

One thing I want to clarify is that you and I don't get to decide who has spiritual authority and who doesn't. On this matter, only God is the one that can know. Even though the kingdom had been taken away from Saul, David still said:

> **And David said to Abishai, Destroy him not: for who can stretch forth his hand against the LORD'S anointed, and be guiltless?**
>
> 1 Samuel 26:9

No one gets to know who the Lord's anointed is and who the Lord's anointed is not. God is the one who grants spiritual authority! It does not come from position, platform, title, seminary, experience, age, rank, popularity etc. Spiritual authority comes from God! Don't get into the mistake of trying to measure it in yourself or others. Even Saul was able to prophesy after the kingdom was taken away from him. We may have gifting's, we may have talents and we may have abilities, but only God knows who has spiritual authority and who does not. Spiritual authority does come from abiding in Christ but it is not something we take; it is something that is given.

It is also important to clarify that spiritual authority is not without its dangers. The nature of spiritual authority is that once it has been granted, it cannot be taken away. **For the gifts and calling of God *are* without repentance** (Romans 11:29). One of the better examples of this is the story of Ananias and Sapphira. The story goes like this:

> **But a certain man named Ananias, with Sapphira his wife, sold a possession, And kept back *part* of the price, his wife also being privy *to it,* and brought a certain part, and laid *it* at the apostles' feet. But Peter said, Ananias, why hath Satan filled thine heart to lie to the Holy Ghost, and to keep back *part* of the price of the land? Whiles it remained, was it not thine own? and after it was sold, was it not in thine own power? why hast thou conceived this thing in thine heart? thou hast not lied unto men, but unto God. And Ananias hearing these words fell down, and gave up the ghost: and great fear came on all them that heard these things. And the young men arose, wound him up, and carried *him* out, and buried *him.* And it was about the space of three hours after, when his wife, not knowing what was done, came in. And Peter**

answered unto her, Tell me whether ye sold the land for so much? And she said, Yea, for so much. Then Peter said unto her, How is it that ye have agreed together to tempt the Spirit of the Lord? behold, the feet of them which have buried thy husband *are* at the door, and shall carry thee out. Then fell she down straightway at his feet, and yielded up the ghost: and the young men came in, and found her dead, and, carrying *her* forth, buried *her* by her husband. And great fear came upon all the church, and upon as many as heard these things.

Acts 5:1-11

Most people teach that this story is meant to invoke the fear of God. The example may include a fear of the Lord element; however, it is my opinion that it shows the dangers involved in having spiritual authority.

An overlooked element of authority is the need for Godly character to back it up. When the soldiers came to arrest Jesus, one of the disciples cut off a soldier's ear. Jesus said "no more of this," and healed the soldier. Luke 9:54 gives a time when Jesus was ministering amongst a people that did not receive him. Several of the disciples said, "Should we call down fire from heaven." Jesus said, "You don't know what spirit you are of." These examples show the need for character amongst the disciples and the Lords desire is not to destroy.

Jesus told us in John 20:23:

Whose soever sins ye remit, they are remitted unto them; *and* whose soever *sins* ye retain, they are retained.

We see that the disciples had the authority to forgive and retain sins. Now look at the story of Ananias and Sapphira and ask yourself a question. Did they die the moment they lied or did they die when Peter retained their sin? Is it possible we have looked at this story backwards for hundreds of years? In one instance, Jesus says to the bloodthirsty disciples, "you don't know what spirit you are of." Now all the sudden people in the new covenant era are being struck dead. Did Jesus change? My personal opinion is that Ananias and Sapphira did sin, but it was Peter's use of authority that got them killed. I know that sounds strange but I believe this example proves we must see spiritual authority as something to respect. It isn't something we should claim inappropriately. It is something that is granted by the Lord as he chooses.

This planet needs to see the people who operate in spiritual authority and it generally comes to those who aren't seeking it.

> **Then there arose a reasoning among them, which of them should be greatest. And Jesus, perceiving the thought of their heart, took a child, and set him by him, And said unto them, Whosoever shall receive this child in my name receiveth me: and whosoever shall receive me receiveth him that sent me: for he that is least among you all, the same shall be great**.
>
> Luke 9:46-48

If we seek spiritual authority rather than relationship with Jesus, the authority we seek will slip through our fingers. If we receive Jesus and his name, we receive him that sent Jesus and we begin the process of abiding. This world needs a generation of people whose shadow delivers from demons. This planet needs to see the sons and daughters of the living God wanting nothing but the Lord Jesus himself, even when man-made kingdoms are thrust upon them. It's only spiritual authority working in our lives that will make a difference to those we minister to; because it's only Jesus that can make any difference in this world. The generation alive today will not be won by men demanding obedience; it will be won by children manifesting the heart of Jesus. We are living in an exciting time in history and in the midst of that excitement, we must understand that the greatest will be the least.

Chapter 15
Relationships

And it was told him by certain which said, Thy mother and thy brethren stand without, desiring to see thee.
And he answered and said unto them, My mother and my brethren are these which hear the word of God, and do it.
Luke 8:20-21

The most important relationship that we will ever have is our relationship with the Lord Jesus Christ. All other relationships, important as they are, must be secondary to our relationship with Him. It is our relationship with the Lord that allows our earthly relationships take on proper meaning. If the Lord is not in his proper place in our hearts, our relationships may begin to degrade into something inhuman, twisted and in some cases demonic.

This isn't to say that relationships with people aren't important. Actually, the Scriptures tell us God's thoughts on relationships when he says:

> **And the LORD God said, *It is* not good that the man should be alone.**
>
> Genesis 2:18

God made man to require and need fellowship, this is a biblical truth. However, God first made us for relationship with him; we see this when the Scripture tells us that God "made man in his own image." We are in the reflection of God and our first relational need is for intimacy with him.

This is hard for some people to accept, especially people that are married and have children. It's difficult to imagine yourself saying that God is most important in my life even above my family. At first this sounds selfish, however the closer we get to God we realize that unless we are abiding in him and his love we won't be able to love our families the way Christ calls us to love them. One of the most startling Scriptures in the New Testament is when Jesus makes the following statement concerning family:

> **If any *man* come to me, and hate not his father, and mother, and wife, and children, and brethren, and sisters, yea, and his own life also, he cannot be my disciple**.
>
> Luke 14:26

Wow! Is Jesus telling us to hate people? No, he is simply saying that he requires that we put him first in all things. This scares some people when they don't understand the nature of God. Most people interpret a Scripture like this with a "religiosity" lens and think God's going to make me do all of these crazy weird things and I'll never get to see my family again. That's not the case at all. Family is of utmost importance to God, otherwise Paul would not have said concerning leaders:

> **(For if a man know not how to rule his own house, how shall he take care of the church of God?)**
>
> 1 Timothy 3:5

God clearly does not want us to forget or hate our families; he just wants our heart of affections turned towards him in all things.

When the void that is meant to be filled up by God is filled up by people, some major distortions can result. One of the most debilitating emotional problems in the world today is the issue of codependency. When our hurt, our pain or our neediness isn't brought to the Lord for healing, it can end in an ungodly attachment to an individual that results in greater harm rather than health. There are clinical definitions to codependency; however, clinical does not necessarily always incorporate spiritual. I believe a good spiritual definition for codependency is: gaining from people what needs to be received from God. A good example of this codependent behavior is seen in the teenage relationship that is so interdependent that jealousy erupts and control sets in whenever someone of the opposite sex comes around. Individuals in this situation are under fear bonds when they act this way. It is by knowing the Lord and what he says about you that you learn your true identity. You don't gain your identity from another person. It is an increasing relationship with Jesus that causes your innermost needs to first be touched by God's love. There is enough of God's love to heal any hurt that has occurred at any level. Relationships will be a part of that healing; however, we must first come to the Lord and surrender our heart to him so that we may receive his love, his kindness and his affections.

Another issue that can result from not placing the Lord first is improper relationship to leaders. The Lord never intended for any leader, spiritual or natural, to take the place of him in our life. In fact, at one point the Lord Jesus said:

But be not ye called Rabbi: for one is your Master, *even* Christ; and all ye are brethren. And call no *man* your father upon the earth: for one is your Father, which is in heaven. Neither be ye called masters: for one is your Master, *even* Christ.

Matthew 23:8-10

Certainly, the Lord does raise up teachers and leaders that minister to us. However, it is the Lord's intent that all of us be firmly fit into Christ "the head," and for us all to be brothers and sisters in the Lord. If we put ministers up on a pedestal and look to them as our connection to the Lord Jesus, then those ministers have become an idol and they have become something the Lord did not intend them to be. A man or a woman on this planet was never meant to stand between you and God. There is only one person who stands between you and the father and that is Jesus. I'm not teaching you to dismiss your leaders and not listen to them. I am saying that it is your calling to come to know the Lord Jesus Christ for yourself.

Some people's relationship with the Lord is so weak and insecure that they will go along with anything someone says or does to them that is supposedly from God. I'm not saying that God won't say or request things that may have a painful element to it, but Paul's rebuke to the Corinthians concerning people was:

For ye suffer (allow it), if a man bring you into bondage, if a man devour *you,* if a man take *of you,* if a man exalt himself, if a man smite you on the face.

2 Corinthians 11:20

Your first relationship is to the Lord Jesus Christ and you must know him in order for all other relationships around you to take shape in a healthy way. This includes what you will and won't do in relationship to those you lead and your leaders.

Once our relationship with the Lord Jesus Christ is properly in place, our relationships with people will take shape healthily. When our relationship with the Lord is in place, we will be able to love others without having neediness added to our love that drains people of their energy. When our relationship with the Lord comes first we will be able to love without unhealthy clinging. When our relationship with the Lord is correct, our friendships will take shape around us in such a way that we won't have to try and they will be healthy. When we understand our relationship with the Lord Jesus Christ, it won't matter if somebody doesn't agree with us. It won't matter if somebody slanders us or does other hateful things to cause harm to us because we know our first love Jesus and that love "compels us." Jesus is our rock! We find our identity and health in Christ. From there our relationships with people take shape and complete the healing. The Lord did create us to need each other and no one will be able to find their destiny without relationships with other people in Christ. However, our first devotion must be to the Lord Jesus Christ and from there our relationships with others take shape in a healthy and godly way.

Chapter 16
The Church

...and upon this rock I will build my church; and the gates of hell shall not prevail against it.
Matthew 16:18b

The special tendency of all old covenant leaders is to enslave its people. This is true of both secular and spiritual arenas. In this structure, people are directed towards leaders rather than the Lord. Though they desire to touch people's lives they will ultimately bind them further because they are not the answer. The scriptures tell us,

> **"Don't you know that whosoever you submit yourself to you become the servant of."**
> Romans 6:16

It is a spiritual principle that you take on the nature of the one you turn yourself over to. If this is a person, you become like them, with their good traits and bad traits. If this is the devil, you become like the devil in thought and action. If it is the Lord, you become like the Lord in his nature.

The tendency of new covenant leaders is to point to Jesus who makes freer and freer. All true shepherds point to the Lord as the answer. True shepherds point to Jesus and teach the sheep how to follow him. They are more concerned with the sheep than the structure the sheep are in. There may be times when a shepherd has many sheep to watch over and times when they have few. Before David was king, his brother prophesied that he only had a "few sheep," to watch over. Regardless of the number, the Lord looks at the heart and the heart of a shepherd is firstly for the sheep (the Church).[6]

The Lord's church is his body. The church is his bride. The church contains the sons and daughters of the living God, "born again" into Christ and now a part of his family. We are his family! We are the bride and Jesus is the bridegroom! The church is made up of individuals who love the Lord Jesus and through that relationship are connected to other lovers of Christ—other lovers of Christ who have become brothers and sisters.

To best understand the church we must identify the foundational biblical principles set forth by Christ in establishing it. It is interesting to note that Jesus did not mention the word church that often. However, his mention of the church sets the foundation of what the church is to become. When Jesus first mentioned the church, he was talking to his disciples and asking them, "who do you say that I am." After Peter responds to the Lord and says, "you are the Christ," Jesus goes on to call Peter blessed and then makes his foundational declaration concerning the church. Jesus said:

---

[6] Moseley, J. Rufus. Manifest Victory. s.l. : Originally printed Harper & Brothers PUBLIC DOMAIN, 1947. p. 207.

> **And I say also unto thee, That thou art Peter, and upon this rock (revelation that I am the Christ) I will build my church; and the gates of hell shall not prevail against it.**
>
> Matthew 16:18

The very first revelation concerning the church is that it would be built on the foundation that Jesus is the Christ. In order for the church to be built in the earth, it must be built on a true revelation of Christ. Many mistakenly allow church to be formed around a perceived assignment or popular teaching. While the assignments the Lord gives us and the teachings of God are important, they are not the Lord himself. In order for the foundation of church to be properly built, it must be built on him. The church is built on the Lord Jesus Christ when we are principally seeking him in all things. If the church is being built on the goods such as prophecy, healing, deliverance, etc., it may be used to fulfill a small function in the body of Christ, but be hindered in terms of its foundations. These gifts are wonderful, but the scriptures teach we can use them and not know Jesus. The church being built on the foundation that Jesus is the Messiah is like the parable of the house that is being built on the rock.

> **Therefore whosoever heareth these sayings of mine, and doeth them, I will liken him unto a wise man, which built his house upon a rock: And the rain descended, and the floods came, and the winds blew, and beat upon that house; and it fell not: for it was founded upon a rock.**
>
> Matthew 7:24-25

The Lord Jesus Christ is our rock and as I have stated, he is also our foundation.

For other foundation can no man lay than that is laid, which is Jesus Christ.
1 Corinthians 3:11

I have seen movements who became built on something like healing, prophecy or ministry to the poor. It is wonderful to be used of the Lord to bring healing. To prophecy and to minister to the poor or any number of wonderful things is a spectacular function. However if we don't clearly seek the Lord as our foundation we can end up unstable in our ministry. I have seen teaching movements that got so enamored with a popular teaching that they forgot to focus on "the teacher," and thus began to have a shaky foundation in their ministry. It is vitally important that this foundational Revelation of Christ not be lost or what is being formed around us cannot be said to be church. It is not knowing the revelation that Jesus is the Christ that causes the church to be formed correctly. It is knowing the revelation of the Christ, that lays the ground work for the church. One is knowledge based and the other is intimacy based. This Christ centered focus is necessary for the church to become what it is called to be.

The next foundation that Jesus mentions concerning the church is that he called it "**my church**." The Lord's church does not belong to any man or woman it belongs to him. In every aspect concerning the church we must seek to know the Lord and what it is that he is saying. We must also place before him anything that we "do" in him and leave it there without feeling possessive of it. One of the number one issues that can take us under in "body life" is the issue of beginning to feel possessive of the Lord's church. The church does not belong to us; we've just seen from the Scriptures it belongs to the Lord and if it belongs to the Lord then there is nothing for us to feel possessive about. If we find ourselves in a situation where we are beginning to feel possessive in our relationships or activities then we have left the simplicity of following Christ in order to build our own kingdom. We don't get to feel possessive concerning the church.

The kingdom of Israel belonged to God; they were God's chosen people. King Saul looked at his own kingship and thought that the Lord's kingdom was actually his and he desperately tried to keep it. The following king, King David, saw the nation of Israel as the Lord's kingdom and he never would cling to it as something he felt possessive over. He felt the kingdom belonged to the Lord. This is why David never tried to obtain a kingly office. This is why David never did anything to strive and try to keep that office. David simply waited on the Lord and operated in the kingly authority that the Lord gave him. He did not exercise an empirical approach to that kingdom, he simply saw himself as a steward of what God had.

If we are to operate in the Lord's church correctly, we must lose every bit of feeling possessive about what belongs to him. We must come to the place where we realize that the church and the kingdom belong to God and there really is nothing that we get to control. So many times we start something with the Lord, but we get into trouble when we start squabbling for "ownership." When the Lord referred to the church he said, "**my church**." There is only one church in the Lord's eyes. The Lord did not say that he would build his churches (plural). He said, "I will build my church." We are not permitted to retain ownership over what we feel the Lord leading us to do. If we are so possessive of our choir programs that we become jealous of another who desires to help, that would tell us we were not building the Lord's church we were building our own kingdom. When we become so possessive of our dance teams, events teams or any other project that getting our way is more important than the Lord having his, we are building our own kingdom. When we start to think of "his" people as "our" people, and feel threatened when they visit other places the church is being formed, we are building our own kingdom. We cannot cling to what belongs to the Lord! We are not permitted to grab hold of anything that is being formed around us except to grab hold of the Lord himself! We are not forever linked even to our "ministries" we are linked to the Lord Jesus and we go and do what we sense he is telling us to go and do. Sometimes many will follow and other times many will walk away; we must follow the Lord!

Think right now of any ministry you are actively involved in. Now imagine a spry, anointed and unseasoned young man or women starts to rise up who is asked to start doing what you are doing as well. If you are noticing jealousy, fear, anger or hatred, it probably means it is time to put that thing on the cross and let the Lord show you where to go from there. I am not saying that there aren't people, who come along with "control problems," who need to be told to just go do something with themselves. When we are focused on the Lord getting his way more than us getting our way, we may be in a place where we tell "controllers" to go spit. However, the danger of that mindset is we often assume that what we want and what God wants are the same and deal with it in a way that makes self-preservation sound spiritual. What we are involved in is not about control problems it is about the Lord being our "head."

The last foundation that we will look at from Matthew chapter 16, is that the Lord Jesus Christ said, "**I will build**." The church is built on the foundation that Jesus is the Christ, it belongs to Jesus and it will be built by Jesus. Because the Lord Jesus has said that he would build his church, it is not necessary for us to focus our attention on building it. We must focus our attention on the building of the Kingdom. Though every believer is a part of the church and will be a part of its formation, it is up to the Lord to form it and we must allow him to be the one in charge of its building.

Many have said that it is our responsibility to build the church because of what the great commission tells us. The great commission says:

> **Go ye therefore, and teach (make disciples of) all nations, baptizing them in the name of the Father, and of the Son, and of the Holy Ghost: Teaching them to observe all things whatsoever I have commanded you: and, lo, I am with you alway, *even* unto the end of the world. Amen.**
>
> Matthew 28:19-20

My response to this concern is that the great commission does not directly discuss the building of the church. The great commission says that through the power and authority of Christ, we are to "go" and make disciples. Most people think that the phrase "go make disciples" means that we are to go make disciples of us, thus building the church. This is an error and in my opinion, a violation of what the Lord Jesus is trying to communicate. The Lord is trying to communicate that he will use us as his hands and feet to make disciples of him. It is not our goal to make disciples and then have them follow us, it needs to be our goal to make disciples of the Lord and show them how to follow him. We are used to build, but what we build is the Kingdom. Once the disciples follow Christ, he will be the one to cause the church to be formed around us. This is the mission set forth in Matthew chapter 28 and at no point does the Lord say go forth and build the church. In reality, the Lord builds his church through people; we are a part of it, but it is still the Lord that builds it.

Others have said that it is our responsibility to build the church because of the Lord's comments concerning the harvest. Matthew 9:37-38 says:

> **Then saith he unto his disciples, The harvest truly *is* plenteous, but the labourers *are* few; Pray ye therefore the Lord of the harvest, that he will send forth labourers into his harvest.**

The common view of this Scripture is that we are building the church and the church should be sending forth laborers. The only problem with this view is that the Lord Jesus Christ told us to pray that the **Father** would send forth laborers. I am not saying that the church won't be involved as senders and harvesters. I am saying that in both instances thus far the Lord Jesus Christ pointed people to himself. We are to pray that Father will send forth Laborers. As our foundations are correctly laid, the church will be built by the Lord nearly automatically. I don't mean to suggest a passive approach to the gospel, just that we must look to the Lord to send us. The Lord may send us through church groups and other relationships, but only he can build his church. The church can be built through missions and it can be built through coffee shop visits. However, our focus is on building his Kingdom not the church. After all, we were told to "**seek first the kingdom**."

The question of where to go from here is the question of how is the church formed? The church is not formed by our attempting to establish it. It is formed by our being established in Christ and our relationship with our brothers and sisters coming together from there.

> **Ye also, as lively (living) stones, are built up a spiritual house, an holy priesthood, to offer up spiritual sacrifices, acceptable to God by Jesus Christ.**
>
> 1 Peter 2:5

When we are brought into the Lord's family, we automatically become part of the church. And it is important to note that first Peter tells us that the church is built of "living stones." Because the church is built of living stones the Lord does not look down from heaven and see multiple sectarian entities, he looks down from heaven and sees one people that are part of his family. Like the scriptures, different churches are actually part of one church (the Lord's), and usually only separated by geography. Church which is separated by geography may easily be referred to as the church in Corinth, the church in Ephesus or the church in Rome.

It wouldn't be prudent to go on from here without answering the question of organizations. All over the world, for thousands of years, the church that Jesus is building has formed in numerous ways. The church has formed alongside of organizations, without organizations (some places its illegal) and in some cases in spite of organizations. There is nothing particularly evil or good about organizations; however, there is a tendency amongst those who see the church as primarily an organization, to start looking at the church with an organizational mindset rather than a relational mindset. This dynamic does not have to exist just because a Christian organization exists. In fact, I know many Christian organizations who have a lively and vibrant manifestation of the Lord's family being formed in their midst. The church can and does exist alongside of organizations. However, the danger exists in beginning to see the organization as the church rather than the people (living stones). Once this jump has been made, the tendency is to begin promoting the organization as what should succeed, rather than the individuals in it being able to step into their calling. Once we see the organization as what needs to succeed, we usually tie God's name to it and pressure people to promote it so it won't fail. Because the success of the church gets tied to an organization, the family dynamic can more easily be relegated to second place. Our goal is to bring people to the Lord, but remember an organization is not God. Coming to a building is not "coming home." We must forget ourselves and show people Christ, "not letting our left hand know what our right hand is doing." We must offer them a hand which speaks of love, not two hands which speaks of building.

When an organizational mindset begins, a hierarchical model is sometimes adopted. There is a tendency, throughout the ages, to re-create structure in church after whatever geopolitical model it is located in. For example, during the age of Kings, the church formed in a structure relatively similar to that of kingship. As a result, the church had popes who led the church as a whole, bishops who led regions and priests who lead people. This is essentially a direct replica of the political environment of their day. In the day that we live in, church has often adopted a makeup which is similar to the political /business environment in the United States. The political arena has the President, Vice President, Cabinet and Joint Chiefs. The business environment has CEOs, CFOs, COO's and Boards. The church organization in the West has Senior Pastors, Associate Pastors, Pastoral Staff and Pastoral Councils (deacons, elders). I'm not suggesting that the structures are necessarily bad in politics and business, in fact certain dynamics require a hierarchical model in order to keep things running smoothly. However, I question the replica of these models in the church. Of course, the tendency will always be to re-create what we have seen. "You are what you eat." However, Christ made numerous statements that would seem to suggest hierarchical was not what he was going for in his church that he is building. Luke 22:24-26 says:

> **And there was also a strife among them, which of them should be accounted the greatest. And he said unto them, The kings of the Gentiles exercise lordship over them; and they that exercise authority upon them are called benefactors. But ye *shall* not *be* so: but he that is greatest among you, let him be as the younger; and he that is chief, as he that doth serve.**

This Scripture is a serious slap in the face to the hierarchical model that exists in some organizational church. This Scripture clearly discusses the issue of Gentile Kings exercising "lordship" over people. Jesus then goes on to say, "But you shall not be so." The Lord Jesus was telling us that he did not want us adopting a lordship model; he wanted the people who desired to be greatest to seek to be the least. Again Matthew 23:8-11 says:

> **But be not ye called Rabbi: for one is your Master, *even* Christ; and all ye are brethren. And call no *man* your father upon the earth:**

for one is your Father, which is in heaven. Neither be ye called masters: for one is your Master, *even* Christ. But he that is greatest among you shall be your servant.

Again we see from this Scripture that the lordship model was not what Jesus desired for his church. The Lord desired people to be directly connected to him and from there the church would be built relationally. Notice the Scripture says not to call anyone Rabbi. Rabbi is really a Jewish term that's similar to the word pastor that we use in the church. How many people have ever heard a teaching that you should not call someone pastor, prophet, teacher etc.? I believe that the Scriptures show that the Lord really never intended for there to be a rigid distance between clergy and laity. We are all meant to be part of the Lord's family and as the Scriptures say we are all "brethren." When we create a hierarchical model in organizational church, we are effectively taking the pharisaical model of religious leadership and copying it. This isn't to say that people won't function as pastors, evangelists, bishop and deacons. The scriptures clearly show these functions; however, I don't see that they are meant to be a hierarchy. Additionally, deacons and elders may be more of a matter of those in a Christian family who are beginning to rise up with passion to teach or go minister. An individual in a church family who takes it upon themselves to begin ministering to the homeless or encouraging other people may easily be referred to as an elder or deacon. This is opposed to a rigid counsel that few are in and most are out. Paul simply instructs us in 1 Timothy to look for certain characteristics in them when they start to rise up in ministry expression.

The church is the body of Christ that is in the earth today. The Lord Jesus Christ is our head. We are his hands and feet. We are meant to be connected to the head so that the actions and work that we do are nearly automatic. Like the relationship between the human brain and the human body. It is through our intimate relationship with the Lord Jesus Christ and relationship with his people that his body, the church, is formed correctly. The church is the Lord's people. To handle them correctly we must remember that there is no man or woman on this earth who gets to the top, it is the Lord Jesus Christ that is at the top and we are the ones that serve. As leaders, it is our job to see that people rise up in their intimacy with Jesus and step forward into their calling. The kingdom is not grown by our putting our own personal agendas first and requiring that people serve them. This leads to a conformity based religion that doesn't set people free. The kingdom is grown by our putting the Lord Jesus Christ first and pointing the way to him with clarity of focus! As we adopt this understanding the church will become more and more the Lord's and less and less ours. As this takes place exponential growth will begin to take place in the body of Christ.

I am not saying any of this with the hope that you will start an internal rebellion in whatever organizational church you attend. Even with all its issues, the church belongs to the Lord and we must honor every leader that the Lord raises up. Even through some of the worst leadership, Daniel was able to thrive with favor from God. So I am not saying you should become negative towards organizations or think all leaders are bad. Most leaders legitimately desire to serve God. Again, organizations exist and are neither good nor bad. There are true expressions of Christ in organizational church and there are true expressions outside it. Don't let anything I'm saying turn you negative towards what the Lord may be doing. If this happens you may end up operating in a religious spirit and tear down what God isn't currently tearing down. Even expressions of church that are way outside what we believe is the correct expression, may still be used by God. If you tear it down you may be making a mistake. No, I am only trying to point out a trend that is present in some expressions of church so that we can avoid this pitfall in ourselves.

The Lord is the one who is building his church, let us look to him to create it and be attuned to the moving of his spirit. It may happen when someone invites you out to lunch. It may happen when a business acquaintance invites you to hear about a struggle he is having. The church may form when you get an email from someone wanting to gather and talk about Jesus. It may happen when you gather to sing songs to the Lord. If you look to Jesus and stay proactive about what he is telling you to do, the church will form regardless of being in a building with a steeple or in a back alley.

Here is a parable from the movie *Dangerous Minds.* A young man has been incredibly wounded by authority. His teacher does everything she can to help him trust her. The young man finally trusts her enough to tell her that he is in some trouble. The teacher tells him he must tell the principle so he can receive protection. Some time passes and the teacher doesn't hear from the young man. She hears on the news that the young man died in an altercation with some dangerous people. The teacher is infuriated and goes to the principle and asks, "What happened? I sent him to you for protection." The principle replied, "I sent him away." The teacher says, "Why did you do that? He came to you for protection." The principle replied, "He opened my door without knocking."

Chapter 17
A Little Leaven

And he charged them, saying, Take heed, beware of the leaven of the Pharisees, and of the leaven of Herod.
Mark 8:15

The Lord Jesus was frequently asked about things which would take place in the future. He was asked questions about recognizing things such as the End Times, the restoration of Israel, his kingdom, etc. In some cases, when the Lord was asked how to discern the times, he responded with ensuring that we could discern the false. As a matter of fact, a substantial portion of the New Testament epistles is devoted to understanding how to recognize that which is false, such as false leaders, false prophets and false ministries etc.

After Jesus had performed the miracles of multiplication, he was walking with his disciples and he made a statement that they did not understand at the time, but has profound repercussions. Jesus turned to his disciples and he said:

> **Take heed, beware of the leaven of the Pharisees, and *of* the leaven of Herod.**
>
> Mark 8:15

After Jesus made this statement the disciples were confused; they thought he was saying something about bread they had forgotten. When Jesus perceived their confusion, he told them that their hearts were hardened and that they had eyes but couldn't see and had ears but could not hear. Jesus wasn't speaking about actual bread; he was using the leaven and bread as an example for his teaching.

Leaven is an ingredient that is added to bread to cause it to rise. Leaven does not add any nutritional value to the food whatsoever; it simply puffs it up. When Jesus was referring to leaven in Mark 8, he was telling us to beware of two things which are "puffed up." Jesus is warning us that there are two things which have an arrogant or prideful base that we must avoid in ourselves and in others or they may cause great harm.

Jesus said, "beware of the leaven of the Pharisees and the leaven of Herod." The similarity between both of these two things is that they were both leaders. Essentially, Jesus was saying, "beware of false leaders." When the disciples could not understand this, Jesus gave the reasoning for their lack of understanding as being a hard heart. Likewise today, these two leavens run rampant throughout much of "body life." The reason for this is likely the same reason Jesus gave that day to his disciples—hardness of heart. It is interesting to note that it is rare to find a teaching in the body of Christ on these two leavens. Could that be a symptom of hardness of heart?

In order to understand the two leavens, we need to look at the two people groups that Jesus was referring to. The Pharisees were a group of "spiritual leaders." However, their spirituality was not in accordance to intimacy with the spirit of God, but duty, obligation, tradition and religiosity. The Pharisees exemplified a false spirituality. The modern understanding of a pharisaical approach to Christianity has become known as the "religious spirit." Herod was not a spiritual leader at all, but rather a kind of governmental leader who sought to advance himself through self-preservation and forming false relationships with important people who could promote him and his agenda. The best way to describe a Herodian approach has become known as the "political spirit." This isn't to say that all politicians are evil; the political spirit is simply a false manifestation of governmental leadership. Another way of saying all of this is, "Beware of that which seems spiritual but is not, and beware of that which seems governmental but is not."

Let's take a closer look at both of these leavens, starting with the leaven of the Pharisees. The leaven of the Pharisees or the religious spirit is a demon which tries to replace the Holy Spirit. In order to do this, it will do or say things which come across as highly "spiritual," and yet it is a false spirituality that does more to distract from the Lord than point to the Lord. Jesus considered the Pharisees to be hypocrites and in one place he says:

> **And when thou prayest, thou shalt not be as the hypocrites *are:* for they love to pray standing in the synagogues and in the corners of the streets, that they may be seen of men. Verily I say unto you, They have their reward**.
>
> Matthew 6:5

The motivation to be seen as "spiritual" is what drives people who have a religious spirit. They will do things that seem spiritual in order to get the attention of men and thus they are distracting attention from the one whom the prayer is for... Christ. Yet another Scripture speaks about this kind of spirit and its tendency to "carry on" in spiritual settings with babblings which are not really of the spirit of the Lord.

> **But when ye pray, use not vain repetitions, as the heathen *do:* for they think that they shall be heard for their much speaking**.
>
> Matthew 6:7

Prayer is wonderful when we are seeking the Lord Jesus and entering into communion with him. However, there is prayer that is rooted in intimacy and prayer that is rooted in spiritual insecurity. One of these opens up the way for the Holy Spirit to begin to move in our midst while the other quenches the Holy Spirit in favor of an individual getting to look spiritual. I've been in situations when I've been ministering under a strong anointing of the Holy Spirit. In the midst of the ministry, I've had individuals come up and began to pray along with me with long-winded babblings and random spiritual sayings or recitations of Scriptures. The result was the Holy Spirit's presence lifted. These individuals are often unaware that there might be a religious spirit in operation because something is driving them to want to get up and do something that seems spiritual. They don't realize what they're doing might cause the presence of the Lord to break. **They have a zeal for God but not in accordance to knowledge**.

I've been in other situations when I've been leading ministry events and the spirit of the Lord would begin moving in power and authority to bring healing and the ministry of prophecy in a mighty way. And yet someone comes to me or someone else in the room and feels like they just have to prophesy; they come up to the microphone and start trying to prophesy, teach, minister and the presence of the Lord breaks totally off of the atmosphere. I won't say that all of these situations were definitely always a religious spirit; however, it's certainly an example of how a religious spirit can operate. It will do anything that it can in order to attempt to replace the Holy Spirit.

Another manifestation of the religious spirit is its tendency to place weights on people that the Lord does not want them to carry.

> **For they bind heavy burdens and grievous to be borne, and lay *them* on men's shoulders; but they *themselves* will not move them with one of their fingers**.
>
> Matthew 23:4

The Lord has born weights for us and it makes no sense to take on false weights, yet the religious spirit attempts to place them on people. The original word for "burdens" in this passage refers to tasks to be performed. What this means is that the religious spirit loves to keep you busy with all kinds of "tasks" or "duties" that are not being done by the unction of the Holy Spirit; they are simply placing heavy loads on people that they cannot bear. Neville Johnson, in his CD-ROM series on Grace, said it best concerning pharisaical burdens when he taught that another word for burdens is an "ideal." Concerning legalism and the religious spirit, Neville Johnson said, "We try and apply the ideal to a situation or circumstance which cannot support that ideal and we become pharisaical placing a load on an individual that they cannot bear and it's biblical."

This type of activity is what the Pharisees specialized in. The Pharisees could quote the Bible up one side and down the other. While the Pharisees could have been considered correct by the letter they were ultimately in error because they were not in accordance with the spirit. I'm not teaching "relativism," it isn't my goal to say that what's right is all relative. What I am saying is that God deals with us as sons and daughters. As a result, the Lord does not require that we be performing perfectly in every area of our life automatically.

If a homosexual is saved and begins to be delivered from their homosexuality, they may not be instantaneously cured. That individual may walk through many years of healing in which the Lord takes them out of that sexual aberration. From time to time, as this individual is walking out their salvation, they may find themselves beginning to slip into old patterns that need to be gently corrected. Pharisees don't understand that God deals with us as sons and daughters and through a process. Pharisees jump on you and use the Bible to kill when the individual falls and does not perform perfectly. The Holy Spirit takes us by the hand, picks us up, sets us back on our feet and gently begins to lead us back on the path we need to be on.

Again, the religious spirit's motivation is to be seen as spiritual and in the process, it cuts the Holy Spirit off from people. Here is Jesus' statement concerning its desire to show a false spirituality.

> **But all their works they do for to be seen of men: they make broad their phylacteries, and enlarge the borders of their garments, And love the uppermost rooms at feasts, and the chief seats in the synagogues.**
>
> Matthew 23:5-6

This next Scripture shows how the religious spirit tries to shut down the move of the Holy Spirit.

> **But woe unto you, scribes and Pharisees, hypocrites! for ye shut up the kingdom of heaven against men: for ye neither go in *yourselves,* neither suffer ye them that are entering to go in.**
>
> Matthew 23:13

The presence of the religious spirit is like a block that tries to prevent the Holy Spirit from moving freely. In many cases, when the Holy Spirit is moving, people may start doing or saying weird things and these can be manifestations of the religious spirit trying to distract us from the Lord.

The religious spirit will use anything it can to prevent the Holy Spirit from being free to move. It will use an emphasis on teaching which does not point to the Lord but rather to the teaching. It will use an emphasis on tradition which cuts off freedom in Christ. It may use manifestations that seem like Holy Spirit manifestations, but there purpose is to distract from the Holy Spirit rather than promote him. I call this a charismatic religious spirit. It may use issues to try to polarize groups of Christians into one category or another. I can tell you without hesitation that being free from the religious spirit has nothing to do with whether or not you drink alcohol. This one issue has polarized Christians in the West more than many others. The truth is you can refrain from drinking and be mostly free from the religious spirit and you can drink and be bound with it. You can also drink and be free or abstain and be bound.

Freedom from the religious spirit means turning to the Lord and fully embracing him and his Holy Spirit in our lives. It also means turning to Jesus for our righteousness rather than personal efforts. As we began to move in intimacy with the spirit of God, we begin to recognize the subtle issues the religious spirit tries to throw at us. As we begin to move in the Holy Spirit, become intimate with him, learn to listen to him and lean into Him, the religious spirit will lose its hold over us and we will begin to embrace a deeper level of freedom in Christ.

The second leaven that Jesus spoke about in Mark 8 is called the leaven of Herod. It is interesting to me that for 25+ years now, the religious spirit (first leaven) has received much attention in the body of Christ. Yet the Herodian (second leaven) or "political spirit," has received hardly any teaching or attention. So many times when I read Mark chapter 8 I find myself thinking about the fact that Jesus mentioned the two leavens and we only seem to focus on the first one. Jesus talked about the leaven of the Pharisees, but he kept talking. We must understand the leaven of Herod if we are to keep from being sidetracked by it. And the political spirit has remained largely hidden.

The leaven of Herod or the political spirit is a demon spirit which seeks to supplant legitimate spiritual authority with illegitimate authority. Similar to how Herod tried to have Jesus destroyed when he was born; a political spirit may strike when God is in the process of raising up a leader who moves in authentic spiritual authority. The goal of this spirit is to politically maneuver itself into positions of visibility within the body of Christ by forming false relationships with prominent individuals or "power" people. Its motivation is territorial advancement. It will attempt to advance in such a way that causes it to be seen as good when in fact its motivations are demonic.

When Jesus was born, Herod the Great was very

much aware of the prophecy concerning the coming King of the Jews. Historically speaking, Herod was not a very nice guy. In fact, history records on multiple occasions that he became convinced members of his own family were out to take his kingdom from him. He became so suspicious and fearful that "his" kingdom was at risk that he ordered many members of his family to be executed. If you do a personal study on Herod, what you will find is self-preservation of the most demonic form. In most cases he became convinced people were after his throne, there wasn't even sufficient evidence to support his theory and yet he had them executed. Herod definitely had some major problems.

Herod was a member of the line of Edomite's. This particular line came from the marriage between Esau and the daughter of Ishmael. Another way of looking at this is to realize that Esau, whom God said he "hated," married the daughter of Ishmael who was the child born of the "slave woman" Hagar. Wow! What a mix to form a genealogy. If ever there was a "redheaded stepchild," this line would be first to claim that undesired title. What is important about all of this is that the roots of Herod's issues come from the lack of legitimacy in that generational line. Herod's generational line was made up of the bringing together of two elements, slavery and hatred. The Edomite line represents a line of people who feel they are not loved by God and have no access to covenant privileges. There is a foundational legitimacy lie and Herod is attempting to compensate for this feeling of lack of legitimacy by amassing political power. The feeling of illegitimacy is at the heart of moving in a Political spirit.

When the wise men that were looking for the Messiah came along, Herod saw an opportunity, and this opportunity becomes the root activity of what we see in the political spirit. Herod sees the wise men coming and sees an opportunity to align himself with them in order to gain what he wants. What Herod wants is information about this King who is to become king of the Jews. At the moment, Herod is a natural king of the Jews and Herod wants to keep his kingdom, hence the self-preservation.

> **Then Herod, when he had privily called the wise men, enquired of them diligently what time the star appeared. And he sent them to Bethlehem, and said, Go and search diligently for the young child; and when ye have found *him,* bring me word again, that I may come and worship him also.**
>
> Matthew 2:7-8

Herod's desire is to kill the child Jesus and he does something twisted that people under a political spirit try to do. Herod aligns himself with the wise men by gaining their trust and getting them to believe that his motives are pure. What I want you to focus on concerning the wise men is that they were highly influential people. What Herod was trying to do was align himself, buddy himself up to or politically maneuver his way into the good graces of these highly important/influential people. He does this fully intending to kill Jesus if he can find him. His motivation is to preserve his kingdom, kill the threat and look like gold in the process. This is essentially how the political spirit operates.

When the political spirit begins to operate in the body of Christ, we usually see this kind of activity taking place. This is why it is so important not to allow someone you don't know to just walk in off the street and immediately be given authority and visibility. People operating in political spirits are master networkers and are frequently able to gain visibility within a few weeks or months. In many cases, they are deceived into believing that the authority they are trying to take is the authority God wants them to have. God may in fact want to give them authority because of the destiny that he has placed on their life but taking it in an illegitimate way will only reap destruction.

Another example of the operation of the political spirit is in one of Herod's children called Herod Antipas. Herod Antipas wanted to marry a woman who was his sister-in-law as well as his niece. As a result of this desired marriage, John the Baptist spoke against it and said that it should not be permitted. Herod wanted to kill what was threatening his plan, but he feared the people because most of them considered John the Baptist to be a prophet. So, he did the next best thing, he had John the Baptist thrown in prison. This is where the situation gets a little bit tricky. What we see next is the political spirit working with the Jezebel spirit in order to gain what it wants.

One night Herod has a party and his wife sends her daughter Herodias in to dance before Herod (Matthew 14:6-11). The motivation for this dance was to get Herod sexually pleased with the site of Herodias and gain his favor in order to get what she wants. This is a straightforward manifestation of what is called the Jezebel spirit. The manipulation, specifically with the sexuality element, is common to Jezebel manifestations. Herod becomes pleased with Herodias and says that he will give her whatever she wants. Now we have the real interesting part, because Herodias mother tells Herodias to ask for John the Baptist's head. Herodias then comes in front of everyone and asks for John the Baptist's head. Now Herod is in the situation of having said he will give Herodias any anything she's asked for and he has to grant the wish. Herod gets John the Baptist's head by partnering with a Jezebel spirit to give it what it wants. Yet again we see the political spirit aligning itself with something that can give it what it wants and it gets to look good in the process. The people think Herod is just being true to his word and so a crisis is adverted.

As I mentioned earlier, the first attack of the political spirit came as the Lord Jesus Christ was born. The Lord's birth indicated the beginning of an era. The birth of a ministry that would bring forth salvation, healings, deliverances, resurrections and a host of other miracles was taking shape. The attack of the political spirit was sent to try to stop it. I've seen these types of manifestations happen within ministries before. I've been in situations where individuals, whom God was raising up with a kind of apostolic authority, are attacked by the political spirit which comes to try to destroy the leader.[7]

Typically what happens is a gifted individual comes in who is good at making quick friendships with powerful people within a church body. This individual begins to promote themselves and their gifts especially with influential leaders within the church. Then the person operating in the political spirit identifies a ministry that it wants to lead or influence. It begins the process of portraying itself as though it would be the logical conclusion of who to be in charge. This may be done with very subtle or highly exaggerated insinuations which are said in front of the people. These insinuations cause people to think the political spirit individual is more mature or gifted than a current

---

[7] Malick, Faisal. The Political Spirit. ebook. Shippensburg : Destiny Image Publishers, Inc, 2008. pp. 41-55. ISBN 10:0-7684-2733-9.

leader. The person with the political spirit will usually seem to humble itself before any leadership that may be over this true leader. This humbling is not done because it's genuine; it is done to try to gain the favor of the people. As this is taking place a hindering spirit is being released against the true leader the Lord is raising up and that individual may find themselves under frequent warfare. By the time the true leader realizes what's going on, he or she may go to their leadership to try to deal with the problem. However, by then the individual with the political spirit has gained the trust of those it wanted to gain. The next step is the leadership tells the true leader that they may have some character issues such as jealousy or an Absalom spirit. This may be done directly or subtly but the sense is the leadership has problems with the true leader now rather than the false. The leadership may encourage the true leader to "get healing," or possibly to step down for a while. All this while, the political spirit individual looks squeaky clean when in fact they are a major source of much of the problem that's taking place. When the true leader is successfully removed, the individual with the political spirit is then free to try and move in.

Both of these character traits, the religious spirit and the political spirit are to be avoided. The Lord Jesus Christ told us to avoid them, he did not want them in us and he did not want us necessarily sitting under them. The way to avoid these issues in our own lives is to constantly submit ourselves before the Lord, learn how to commune with the Holy Spirit and never do anything to promote ourselves or our agenda. It is our job to have no agenda but the Lord's agenda. This does not mean that we can allow ourselves to be deceived into thinking that our agenda is the Lord's. We must allow the Lord to be the one to make his will known without tainting it with our subtle opinions and agendas. The best advice that I can give is not to seek spiritual authority at all, but rather seek the Lord first and only accept authority when it is thrust on you and you can't get rid of. The Lord Jesus Christ did not go around concerned about whether people were listening to him or not. The Lord Jesus Christ simply did what he saw the Father doing and allowed the chips to fall where they may. Like the Lord, it is our job to scatter seed and is not our job to be concerned as to what type of ground it is falling on. The condition of the ground the seeds are falling on is between the ground and the Lord.

Beware of the leaven of the Pharisees and of the leaven of Herod in yourself and in others. Don't operate in suspicion having learned what you've learned. If your heart is pure the Lord will help you know what you should do. Suspicion is only a manifestation of the same spirit you're trying to avoid. If you see someone operating like this, ask for counsel from those you trust outside the group and seek the Lord. Do not try to take over a ministry or get everyone to listen to you, that is a form of false leadership as well. You are responsible for you! Operate in love and only seek to be intimate with the Lord and help others be intimate with the Lord. This is the essence of apostolic authority.

Chapter 18
Destiny

And the angel answered and said unto her, The Holy Ghost shall come upon thee, and the power of the Highest shall overshadow thee:
Luke 1:35a

Everyone is born with a unique destiny granted from the Father. Many people struggle with the concept of destiny because they don't understand their purpose. Your purpose is made up of the unique ingredients Jesus has placed in you. Over the course of your life, Jesus will draw you into his presence and pull on each ingredient. This will ultimately lead you to want to use your specific ingredients. Ministering to Jesus and using the gift mix Jesus has placed in you for His Kingdom is your calling. Following Jesus and his calling is what leads you to your destiny.

The truth is that your calling is unique to you and you are totally incapable in yourself of fulfilling that calling. Like the story of Gideon who was completely incapable to lead an army, God chooses people who have particular purposes that are much higher than their natural ability to attain. God does this so that he may show himself strong in our lives and we may know that it truly is all about God. This is a completely separate method than the one the world uses. Worldly systems often look for the most capable, experienced and likely to succeed. God, on the other hand, looks for the one who carries a deposit on their life. A David who may have no experience. The deposit that I speak of is God's fingerprint on a life and it is called destiny.

One of the neatest examples of destiny in the Scriptures is seen in the life of Mary the mother of Jesus. Mary was a young woman who was pure, never married and favored in the sight of the Lord. One day, an angel showed up and told her that she was going to give birth to a son and that son would be the Christ. Imagine being a young teenager and having this kind of God encounter. Mary was engaged to be married and had never been with a man but she was told by the angel that she would bear a child by the power of the Holy Spirit. This meant that Mary would have to bear extraordinary reproach amongst her people. Imagine someone coming up to you today and telling you that they're having a child and oh by the way it happened supernaturally. Most people would not believe you! However Mary did have that child, she did name him Jesus and through all that she went through the Lord did his part to fulfill her destiny.

Mary's example of finding her destiny appeals to us all. As we take a closer look at the events leading up to her destiny to give birth to the Christ, we get a closer look at how our destiny unfolds. Obviously there will be some differences seeing as how there won't be a need for an immaculate conception. However, there are principles in the life of Mary that we can draw upon to see how our own destiny will take shape.

The first thing that we must look at in the life of Mary is the favor that she walked in.

> **And the angel came in unto her, and said, Hail, *thou that art* highly favoured, the Lord *is* with thee: blessed *art* thou among women.**
>
> Luke 1:28

Mary had found favor in the eyes of the Lord and this unction of favor from God allowed her to move towards her destiny. Likewise it is favor from God which causes us to be led into our destiny. Through the finished work of the Lord Jesus, every believer has as much if not more favor than Mary did. Mary was born of woman before the finished work of the cross and concerning this, the Lord Jesus Christ said:

> **Verily I say unto you, Among them that are born of women there hath not risen a greater than John the Baptist: notwithstanding he that is least in the kingdom of heaven is greater than he.**
>
> Matthew 11:11

Since every believer in Christ gets brought into the kingdom of God, every believer is greater than Mary. As such, as believers you and I have enough favor for our destiny to be fulfilled as Mary the mother of Jesus had. I might add at this moment that I do not see Mary as a divinity as some do; I see her as a person who was chosen by God to help fulfill his purposes. Luke 1:28 can very well be foreshadowing the favor that you and I would have in Christ. It could easily be said of us that we are, "highly favored," "in the presence of the Lord," and "blessed." The key here is that we choose to believe that we are blessed in Christ Jesus. No matter what our feelings seem to dictate, our favor and blessing come from Christ Jesus and are secured in his finished work. Therefore, the favor that we need to step into our destiny has already been released.

The next thing that we must see is that fear is the enemy of our true destiny and like Mary, we are encouraged not to tolerate it.

> **And the angel said unto her, Fear not, Mary: for thou hast found favour with God.**
>
> Luke 1:30

As we see here, fear is one of the attacks the enemy uses to try to block destiny. Our blessing, favor and destiny come from God and the enemy knows that. There is nothing the enemy can do to remove the favor that you already have in Christ. As we discovered, favor is established through the finished work of Jesus on the cross. If the enemy can get you to doubt that favor and begin to operate out of fear, it is the only way he can push you back. We must remember the instructions the angel gave Mary, "you have found favor with God." It is God that is with you and it is God that goes before you and the enemy is nowhere near as strong as God. Walking into your destiny is an opportunity for you to learn that God is bigger than the devil. Sure the devil may try to attack you but those attacks don't represent who you are they represent the evil that he is. You aren't fearful, it's the devil that's fearful. It is a spiritual principle that you can only use as a weapon that which you have in your arsenal. The devil can only use fear because he is afraid. Godly men and women need not use fear on people because fear is not a part of their arsenal. The major weapon of our arsenal is love, joy, peace, patience and all the fruits of the spirit. If the enemy attacks you with a hindrance just say out loud, "in Jesus name I refuse this hindrance."

The next step in walking into your destiny is to understand that the Lord gives you a destiny that he first forms within you and then releases through you.

And, behold, thou shalt conceive Luke 1:31

It is the Lord who teaches you and causes the makeup of your destiny to be built within you. Your truest destiny is to live in Christ and allow him to live in you. This literally happened in the case of Mary; however, it is the Lord that comes to live in the heart of every believer. As a relationship with the Lord unfolds your giftings and talents and the purposes that he is causing to unfold within you will begin to rise up to the surface. As your giftings rise up and favor increases you will begin to see the destiny that will turn into your life's call.

After our destiny has been conceived and is being pulled towards the surface, it is a temptation to get anxious and ask the Lord "how." How do I do this? What am I supposed to do? This is a very common stage to go through and even some of the most spiritual giants in the word of God struggled with.

Then said Mary unto the angel, How shall this be, seeing I know not a man?

Luke 1:34

When Abraham was promised to be a great nation and yet had no children, he wanted to know how it would take place and so he cut corners and lay with his servant Hagar. Similarly Mary wanted to know how all of this was to take place and it is a question that we will likely struggle with.

The answer to the how question is that it will be done through the power of the Holy Spirit.

> **And the angel answered and said unto her, The Holy Ghost shall come upon thee, and the power of the Highest shall overshadow thee**:
>
> Luke 1:35

Your destiny can only be fulfilled through the Holy Spirit. There is no earthly technique, model or system that can make your God-given destiny come to pass. It takes something of heaven for your heavenly purpose to be revealed. Likewise, the Holy Spirit is the key to unlocking everyone's individual destiny. It is more important to sit in the presence of the Holy Spirit than it is to understand an earthly model. It is more important to abide in the presence of God than it is to be friends with kings and presidents. Your destiny is not wrapped up in what you can do; it's wrapped up in what he can do. You may be able to learn organizational skills and other business commodities, however the truth of your destiny still stands. "The Holy Ghost shall come upon you and the power of the highest shall overshadow you." Techniques are not the answer. Networking ability is not the answer. The answer is a person named Jesus and you know him through the power of the Holy Spirit.

The last step you must take in going the pathway of your destiny is the path of saying yes to all of this.

> **And Mary said, Behold the handmaid of the Lord; be it unto me according to thy word. And the angel departed from her**.
>
> Luke 1:38

It takes courage to choose to trust the Lord to fulfill your destiny the way he wants to do it. For most it is easier to go to college, get a degree and try to network your way to the top of something. This isn't to say that the Lord may not send people to college, tell them to get a degree or use godly relationships to help them reach their destiny. It is to say that the best way, the highest way is the path of knowing the Lord in his presence. You can't become familiar with the healing presence of the Lord unless you personally spend time in his healing presence. You can't become familiar with the loving presence of the Lord enough to love others into the kingdom, unless you've spent time in the loving presence of the Lord Jesus. It's hard to choose to go down this path! Everything in society tells you that it's better to go down the path of self-gain. However, the pathway the Lord has chosen for you is the pathway of presence.

Chapter 19
Rest

Come unto me, all ye that labour and are heavy laden, and I will give you rest.
Matthew 11:28

Think about what it's like to work one year solid with no break. Think for a minute about how you start to feel about your job, your friends and every day activities. For most people the stress begins to mount and other areas of life began to suffer. Now imagine that feeling you get when you cut ties with your job, get in the car with your family and start heading down to the beach. Maybe you roll down the window and embrace the exhilaration of the wind blowing in your face mixed with the knowledge that there is nowhere you have to be. There's nowhere you have to be because the obligations you are under have been removed. Most Christians live their lives the first way; the way of feeling burdened down with weights and obligation. However, the second way is the way Christians are called to live in terms of their spirituality. The second way is the way of rest.

One of the most necessary ingredients in the Christian life is the element of rest. Rest was created by God on the seventh day of creation and it was the very first thing that God sanctified.

And on the seventh day God ended his work which he had made; and he rested on the seventh day from all his work which he had made. And God blessed the seventh day, and sanctified it: because that in it he had rested from all his work which God created and made.

Genesis 2:2-3

Since God sanctified rest, it is necessary for the believer to operate from a place of rest in all that they do. Rest isn't just an option we have to take from time to time, it is a sanctified truth we are called to live in. Since God rested and sanctified rest, it takes rest to be able to connect with the spirit of God. Since Jesus finished his work on the cross and "sat down," at the right hand of the father; Jesus has rested from his finished work and it takes an attitude of rest to connect with him at a deep level.

One day Jesus was ministering and he announced that he was the source of rest and that by coming to him we can begin to enter in to the experience of rest.

Come unto me, all *ye* that labour and are heavy laden, and I will give you rest.

Matthew 11:28

This reveals to us that there is no true rest apart from Jesus. This also reveals that as we come to him, a symptom that we are encountering the Lord is greater and greater rest. If we're not experiencing a rest in our spiritual life that seems to be getting deeper every day, we have fallen off track somewhere and we need to follow Jesus back to the place of ever increasing rest.

Jesus continues his instruction by telling us that his way to rest is by taking his yoke.

Take my yoke upon you. Matthew 11:29a

Most people interpret a passage like this through the lens of religion. By this I mean, they feel they're supposed to be weighed down with obligations that Jesus gives them in order to be obedient to him. In so, they turn a verse that was meant to free us into a verse that instructs people how to become further bound. They take freedom and exchange it for obligation to man. I'm not saying that if you have a boss you shouldn't do what they ask you to. However, the Lord's instruction was not to take the yoke of man it was to take "his" yoke upon you. This means that you are yoked to Jesus in your life. There is a godly joining "yoking" that happens between husband and wife, however there really is no call other than this in the word to be yoked to people, places or things. You are yoked to Jesus! Jesus goes on to tell us:

For my yoke *is* easy, and my burden is light. Matthew 11:30

A yoke is a harness that goes around an animal which is pulling the weight of something. When these types of yokes were used the lesser strength animal was invariably linked or "yoked," to the greater strength animal. This is a picture of what this means for us as believers. Jesus is the greater strength and by our being yoked to him, we are yoked to his strength, grace, peace, joy, ability and freedom, etc.

Since it is our gift to be able to come to the Lord to receive rest, we must understand the source of what it is that makes us weary. Jesus instructed us to take his yoke, from this we can assume that a primary source of weariness is taking yokes which we are not designed to take. As I have mentioned, the yoke we are to take is the Lord's yoke. However, people are frequently weighed down with yokes to people, places and things. These yokes rob them of their rest and their simple ability to abide in the presence of the Lord.

One of the most common things people get yoked to is Christian service. If the Lord is speaking to you to do a particular thing, then there is a grace that goes along with that thing. Whatever it is the Lord is asking you to do will be a joy for you because he places his desire in your heart. I'm not saying that there aren't difficulties that Christians run into. However, even in the midst of tremendous persecution, it can be a delight to do what he gives you to do because anything you do with him is a joy. If you are in the midst of all of your Christian "doings," and you find yourself losing rest, then it is a pretty good sign you have become yoked to something you did not need to become yoked to.

Another example of what we can be yoked to is people and places. Remember we are yoked to a person but that person is Jesus. Often people become yoked to pastors, teachers, businesses and church organizations without realizing it. By taking on the yoke of these people and places, they lose sight of the simplicity of devotion to Jesus. Then they find themselves in a swirl of activity that's putting more weight on their already burdened lives. I've lost track of the number of pastors I've spoken to who no longer have any time to spend with their families because they're so weighed down with obligations.

Remember Jesus warning in Matthew chapter 7 when he said:

> **Many will say to me in that day, Lord, Lord, have we not prophesied in thy name? and in thy name have cast out devils? and in thy name done many wonderful works? And**

then will I profess unto them, I never knew you: depart from me, ye that work iniquity.
Matthew 7:22-23

The Lord wants intimacy with us. Relationship with Jesus is the key. Actions will come as we walk with and yield to God. But as we've just seen, putting the cart before the horse can be dangerous in Christian life.

The way to keep from taking yokes we are not designed to carry is to know the Lord. When Jesus began to teach that all who are weary and burdened should come to him he said:

...learn of me; for I am meek and lowly in heart: and ye shall find rest unto your souls.
Matthew 11:29

We are invited by Jesus to learn about him. This learning takes place by connecting with him intimately. As we connect with Jesus in the secret place, the heavy yokes and burdens will begin to drop. As we gaze into the face of our Savior, we see him more clearly and we see that he has carried every burden for us. The real work has already been done and we get to rest in its completion. It is our delight to "look unto Jesus, the author and finisher of our faith." Jesus is the one who authors and he is the one who finishes, this means he starts the work, does the work and completes the work.

If you are under heavy burdens in your life, then the best thing to do is to come to the Lord Jesus and surrender everything at his feet. The Lord will show you how to set things down that he doesn't want you to carry. Again, I am not saying that people should just sit around and do nothing all the time. Christians who are led by the spirit of God will be involved in activities that the spirit of the Lord leads them to do. At times this will involve what groups are doing, at times this may involve what organizations are doing, at times it may involve what just you and your spouse are doing and at times it may involve what you and the Lord are doing. However, if you become yoked to something where it is an obligation for you to do things rather than the joy of the Lord for you to do, you have likely taken something on yourself that you were not designed to carry. I imagine the cross Jesus had to carry up to Calvary was a pretty heavy burden to lift, but he carried it. The work is done. Turn to Jesus and learn of him. Set down the heavy burdens that are robbing you of your joy. It's time for the people on earth to rise up who are first and foremost yoked to the Lord.

Chapter 20
Open Heavens

And he saith unto him, Verily, verily, I say unto you, Hereafter ye shall see heaven open, and the angels of God ascending and descending upon the Son of man.
John 1:51

Have you ever been outside on a sunny day only to be surprised by a sudden heavy rain? I've always found something exhilarating about a sudden downpour. One minute you're going about your business and the next minute your soaking wet! One thing's for certain, when you find yourself under the skies water faucet, your plans change. You may have to reschedule meetings, show up late or alter life altogether. This is what happens when you find yourself standing under the force of rain coming down from the heavens. This is also what it's like when we come to the revelation of the nature of Jesus and the open heaven that we walk-in.

Like the natural rain, the revelation that we walk in an open heaven is meant to change everything. Just like being drenched with rain, we have become drenched in the presence of the Lord Jesus. This presence causes life to change! The presence of God raining down on us may cause us to change careers, cancel meetings, show up late for events or any number of things that we can't foresee. This is because those who are under the force of God's presence are "like the wind, you don't know where they're coming from or where they're going." They aren't tied to things that have become idols, they are tied to the presence of the Lord Jesus Christ and everything they do stems from that.

When Jesus first met Nathaniel, his conversation with him revealed something about the nature of Jesus that we all get to walk in. Jesus reveals his identity to Nathaniel by telling him that he prophetically saw him while Nathaniel was under a tree. Nathaniel was moved by this and began to understand that this Jesus was in fact the son of God. Then Jesus says something to Nathaniel that is foundational to our understanding. Jesus said:

> **Because I said unto thee, I saw thee under the fig tree, believest thou? thou shalt see greater things than these. And he saith unto him, Verily, verily, I say unto you, Hereafter ye shall see heaven open, and the angels of God ascending and descending upon the Son of man**.
>
> John 1:50-51

Jesus has just promised Nathaniel that he would see the heavens opened and the angels of God ascending and descending upon the Son of Man. In other words, Jesus has just promised Nathaniel that he would get to see a time of open heavens. The disciples will get to see the healings, miracles, deliverances and other expressions of the power Ministry of heaven due to the heavens being open.

Nathaniel's experience speaks of another experience that Jacob had back in the book of Genesis. Scripture records the following story about Jacob:

And Jacob went out from Beersheba, and went toward Haran. And he lighted upon a certain place, and tarried there all night, because the sun was set; and he took of the stones of that place, and put *them for* his pillows, and lay down in that place to sleep. And he dreamed, and behold a ladder set up on the earth, and the top of it reached to heaven: and behold the angels of God ascending and descending on it. And, behold, the LORD stood above it, and said, I *am* the LORD God of Abraham thy father, and the God of Isaac: the land whereon thou liest, to thee will I give it, and to thy seed;

Genesis 28:10-13

As you can see this is not the first time this encounter was mentioned. However, the first experience depicts Jacob and what he sees coming down from heaven is a ladder. This ladder reaches up into heaven in the first experience but the second experience does not mention the ladder. The Nathaniel experience says that the angels will be coming and going on Jesus. Since the Genesis experience depicts a ladder and John chapter 1 mentions everything but the ladder, we can assume that the ladder is Christ.

The purpose and function of a ladder is to support one while they are ascending or descending it. Since Jesus tells Nathaniel that he is the ladder, we see that Jesus is the source of open heavens and the way for us to come up higher.

Since Jesus is the ladder and the angels are ascending and descending upon him, then the same realm of freedom that Christ walked in has been opened to us because Jesus is in our hearts. Since Jesus lives in us, the heavens are opened above us because they are opened above the Lord. Since Jesus lives in us, the angels are ascending and descending on us all the time. The result is the same freedom to operate in the ministry of heaven that Jesus had is available to every believer. The same bountiful gifts of heaven to move in healing, prophecy, faith, miracles and all the rest are available for you and me now!

Jesus walks in a consistent open heaven and the result is that we get to walk in a consistent open heaven. As a matter of fact, the result of Christ's finished work is that we have been "**seated with him, in him, in heavenly places**." No matter what we may feel like on any given day, we have already been seated with Jesus in heaven. Because our mission from the Lord's prayer is, "on earth as it is in heaven," our mission is to operate in the heavenly and release the heavenly everywhere we go. The result is a presence of God driven life!

Jesus lives in you! His presence is in you and around you. All that he is has become available to you. Our gift is to come to Christ and through intimacy with him move higher up the ladder. This isn't to imply that there are some Christians who are higher or lower in the food chain than others. However, in any relationship it's possible for someone to know an individual better than someone else knows them. As we move deeper into intimacy with him, his presence, the realm of heaven and the ministry of the angels become more real to us and we begin to move on earth as it is in heaven.

Jesus is the way! He is the path we start down, he is the path we are on and when we reach the end, we will find him there, too. Our whole lives and everything that we are is meant to be summed up in Jesus. Our purpose is to fully surrender and yield to him and experience the joy and liberty of his life being lived through us. As we touch this life, as we believe this is possible we step into a realm of the unknown where "**the blind see, the deaf hear and the dead are raised**." We step into a realm where we hear Jesus say to us:

> **Verily, verily, I say unto you, Hereafter ye shall see heaven open, and the angels of God ascending and descending upon the Son of man.**
>
> John 1:51

Chapter 21
In the Name of Jesus

And whatsoever ye shall ask in my name, that will I do, that the Father may be glorified in the Son.
John 14:13

As we've seen the whole spiritual life is about intimately knowing Christ and then seeing him manifest through us. When we come to the Lord Jesus, we begin to see him as he is and our understanding of him is transfigured before us. As he's transfigured before us we are changed by beholding him with an unveiled face. As we look unto Jesus the author and finisher of our faith, we are changed because of that spiritual law that says: you become like what you look at. We can't look at the Lord and not be changed! His radiance, the fire in his voice and the warmth of his embrace are an all-encompassing experience. As we are experiencing him, he begins to experience us and the two began to become one in the presence of the Lord. Yes, we are still an individual, he doesn't remove that from us but a joining takes place that's deeper and more intimate than a natural marriage can make possible.

As the Lord's presence saturates us, we become carriers of something holy. We become carriers of the glory of God. God's glory and his characteristics are mixed. When Moses asked God if he could see his glory, God's response was:

> **And he said, I will make all my goodness pass before thee, and I will proclaim the name of the LORD before thee; and will be gracious to whom I will be gracious, and will shew mercy on whom I will shew mercy.**
>
> Exodus 33:19

God's response to Moses was that he would cause his goodness to pass before him. From this we see a tie between glory and goodness, between presence and characteristics. God's glory is his love, God's glory is his grace, God's glory is his goodness and it is wrapped up in the name of the Lord. Notice God said, "I will proclaim the name of the Lord before thee." God's glory is his nature and his characteristics are released through his name.

As we carry the glory of the presence of the Lord in our lives, the name of the Lord is proclaimed before us. As the Lord is built into us, his very nature permeates us and a greater measure of his name is present. Jesus instructed us to pray to the father in the name of the Lord Jesus.

> **And whatsoever ye shall ask in my name, that will I do, that the Father may be glorified in the Son.**
>
> John 14:13

Therefore we come to a place in our walk with God where everything we do we do in the name of Jesus. We understand that his name, his glory and his characteristics are all tied together. As a result of his presence increasing on our lives, we become carriers of his name and his glory. When we pray, we are to pray in the name of Jesus. When we go, we are to go in the character and nature of Jesus. When we sing, we are to sing in the presence and the name of Jesus. As we bask in the glory of his name, we see his presence reaching out beyond us to permeate all that is around us.

The nature of Jesus is to be a healer, so when we enter his presence we enter healing and yes we enter the name of Jesus. The nature of Jesus is to be full of light so when we enter his presence darkness departs from us and it goes in the name of Jesus. The nature of Jesus is to be full of life and resurrection power, so when we enter his presence death departs and we are resurrected in the name of Jesus.

Some have treated the name of Jesus like a trinket or a charm that we tack on to the end of a prayer. We use his name like a passcode and sit around and wonder if it's going to work or not. Of course we are to pray in the name of Jesus but it's more than that. We are to come to the Father in the name of Jesus. As we receive the Lord Jesus and learn to abide in his love, presence and glory, we come to the Father bearing the name of Jesus. When we pray, we pray in the name of Jesus and the Father moves because of that name.

The whole of our life is about turning to the Lord and becoming more intimate with him. The whole of our life and its turning is turning to the name of Jesus. When we need his hand to reach into her heart and bring healing to our lives we turn to the name of Jesus. When our brother won't speak to us and all we know to do is to come and wash their feet, we do so in the name of Jesus.

Turn to the Lord Jesus Christ! Be patient in his presence and allow his glory to be built into you. Let his presence wash over you and change you because his presence is the only thing that ever will. Learn to rest, learn to abide in his love and learn to trust him. And as you go, go forth in the name of Jesus!

About the Author

Jonathan Hogan is a husband, father, author, minister, singer, songwriter and lover of Jesus Christ. Jonathan is based out of Birmingham, Alabama where he ministers itinerantly at churches, conferences, small groups, home groups and other events. His ministry focus is geared towards helping people become intimate with the Lord Jesus, walk in personal freedom and step into their calling.

Jonathan fulfills his focus by leading people into an atmosphere of the Presence of God. His ministry takes the form of prophetic ministry, worship, song of the Lord, teaching and praying for the release of God's healing power. His teachings focus on Intimacy with Jesus, the Kingdom of Heaven and how believers may "know the Lord and do great exploits."

Jonathan's background is rich in biblical studies, ministry training and personal intimacy with the Lord Jesus Christ. As a young man Jonathan studied and graduated from Briarwood Christian School. By the time he graduated high school he had completed extensive training in Old and New Testament studies, Interpretation, In-depth study of the New Covenant Gospels and Epistles, Marriage and Family studies, Introduction to Systematic theology, and more.

In the year 2000 he encountered the manifest presence of the Lord Jesus Christ. After this initial encounter with the Lord his entire life changed and he began to seek the Lord in private for hours every day. During this season Jonathan feels he met the God of the Bible in a profound way and it has affected everything in his life ever since. Jonathan has since felt delivered from his overly dogmatic early years and is joyful in knowing Jesus as a living breathing Lord rather than an impersonal God studied in a classroom. In addition to receiving his bachelors degree in music from the University of Southern Mississippi, Jonathan has received continued training in Biblical foundations, prophetic ministry, inner healing prayer, teaching and prayer for physical healing. He has understudied under such ministers as Charles Kraft (fuller theological), Judy Taber (Hearts Set Free International Ministries) and Elaine Gentry (Tender Mercies Ministries).

Between 2006 and 2014 Jonathan pastored an evening service in which the presence of the Lord was made the central focus and the miraculous touch of God moved in great strength for deliverance, healing and prophecy. Through these ministry nights the Lord began to move him into an individual ministry as well as corporate church ministry. Jonathan's passion for intimacy with Jesus has led him to focus his attention on walking in the abiding presence of the Holy Spirit.

Jonathan's background has given him understanding how religious spirits seek to hinder Gods people from intimacy with Him. Removing false religious burdens is a strong theme of Jonathans teaching. Jonathan believes that it is vital for the body of Christ to "know their God" and once they know him they will "do great exploits". Dan 11 (healing, signs, wonders). He believes there has been a lot of teaching about doing things for God (religious focus) but not much understanding exists on how to shift into intimately knowing him (Grace Focus).

Additionally, hearing God, waiting on God, seeking God, the love of God and walking with God are strong themes in his ministry. He believes that the relationship is the gateway to doing things the Lord is leading.

WWW.JONATHANHOGAN.ORG

13458161R00088

Printed in Great Britain
by Amazon.co.uk, Ltd.,
Marston Gate.